engag[e]

Starter

Student Book

Gregory J. Manin   Alicia Artusi

OXFORD
UNIVERSITY PRESS

Contents

Welcome

Sign in

1 Write your name and a password.

2 Write some English words you know.

CD, hip hop, …

Numbers 1–20

1 Match the numbers with the words.

0 1 2 3 4 5 6 7 8 9 10 11 12 13 14 15 16 17 18 19 20

two three five one sixteen eleven fifteen fifteen four nine seventeen fourteen thirteen six seven nineteen twelve eighteen zero ten eight

Now listen and repeat.

2 Listen and repeat the pairs of numbers.

1	11	2	12	3	13
4	14	5	15	6	16
7	17	8	18	9	19

3 Listen to the numbers. Write the next number in the sequence.

1 *five*
2 ________
3 ________
4 ________

Colors

1 Label the numbers with the words below.

red blue orange yellow black
brown green pink white purple

4 *black*
16 ________
12 ________
9 ________
18 ________
19 ________
5 ________
11 ________
20 ________
13 ________

Now listen and repeat.

2 Fill in the blanks with the correct color.

1 Four is *black*.
2 Sixteen is ________.
3 Twelve is ________.
4 Nine is ________.
5 Eighteen is ________.
6 Twenty is ________.
7 Five is ________.
8 Eleven is ________.
9 Twenty is ________.
10 Thirteen is ________.

3 Complete this sentence.

My favorite color is ________________.

Now tell the class.

Classroom objects

1 Label the objects with the words below.

ruler eraser pencil
notebook pen desk

🎧 **Now listen and repeat.**

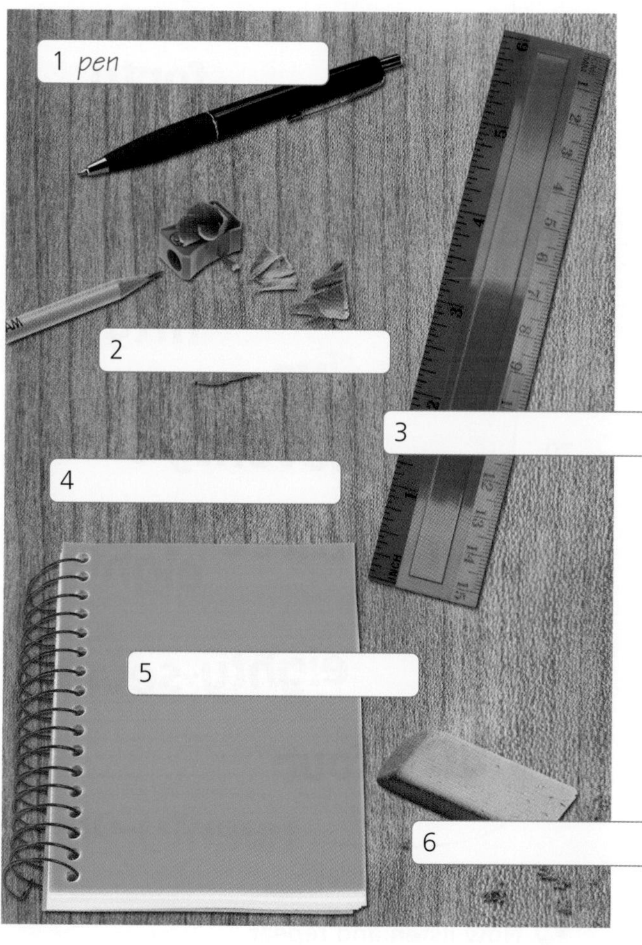

2 Ask and answer in class.

The alphabet

1 🎧 Listen and repeat.

a b c d e f g h i j k l m n o p q r s t u v w x y z

2 🎧 Listen and repeat.

/eɪ/	/i/	/e/	/aɪ/	/ou/	/u/	/ar/
a	b	f	i	o	q	r
h	c	l	y		u	
j	d	m			w	
k	e	n				
	g	s				
	p	x				
	t					
	v					
	z					

3 🎧 Listen and repeat.

1 **A E I O U**
2 **U A O I E**
3 **O I E U A**

4 🎧 Listen. Circle the letter you hear.

1 (A) E
2 E I
3 G J
4 I Y
5 V B
6 P B

5 Ask and answer in class.

1 How do you spell your first name?
2 How do you spell your last name?

6 Ask and answer about classroom objects.

Student A: How do you spell pen?
Student B: P-E-N.

Days of the week

1 Listen and repeat.

Monday Tuesday Wednesday Thursday
Friday Saturday Sunday

2 Fill in the blank.

Today is ______________.

3 Listen to the days. Write the missing day.

1 *Wednesday*
2 ______________
3 ______________
4 ______________

Months of the year

1 Listen and repeat.

My class birthday calendar

January	February	March	April
May	**June**	**July**	**August**
September	**October**	**November**	**December**

2 Answer the teacher.

Teacher: When's your birthday?
Student A: In July.
Write the names in the calendar.

3 Look at the birthday calendar. Ask and answer in class.

Student A: Pedro
Student B: July

Numbers 20–100

1 Match the numbers with the words.

21
30
32
40
43
50
54
60
65
70
76
80
87
90
98

thirty
seventy
ninety
thirty-two
sixty
forty
a hundred
ninety-eight
fifty
sixty-five
seventy-six
forty-three
eighty
eighty-seven
fifty-four
twenty-one

Now listen and repeat.

2 Listen. Write the numbers you hear.

90, ___, ___, ___, ___, ___, ___, ___, ___.

3 Write the numbers using words.

1 The number of students in your class.
____
2 The number of classrooms in your school.
____
3 The number of teachers in your school.
____
4 The number of boys in your class.
____
5 The number of girls in your class.
____

Classroom language

1 Write the correct question in the speech bubble.

What does 'pencil' mean? Can you repeat that, please? How do you say this in English?
What page is it? How do you spell 'pen'?

1 *How do you spell 'pen'?*
P-E-N.
2
Pencil!
3
Page 22.
4
Page 22.
5

Now listen and repeat.

Bingo

1 Fill in the board. Then play bingo with the class.

Number 1–20	Number 21–40	Number 41–60	Number 61–80	Number 81–100
day	day	day	day	day
color	color	color	color	color
month	month	month	month	month

1 Identity

Grammar: *be* (affirmative); *be* (questions)
Vocabulary: countries; nationalities

Exploring the topic

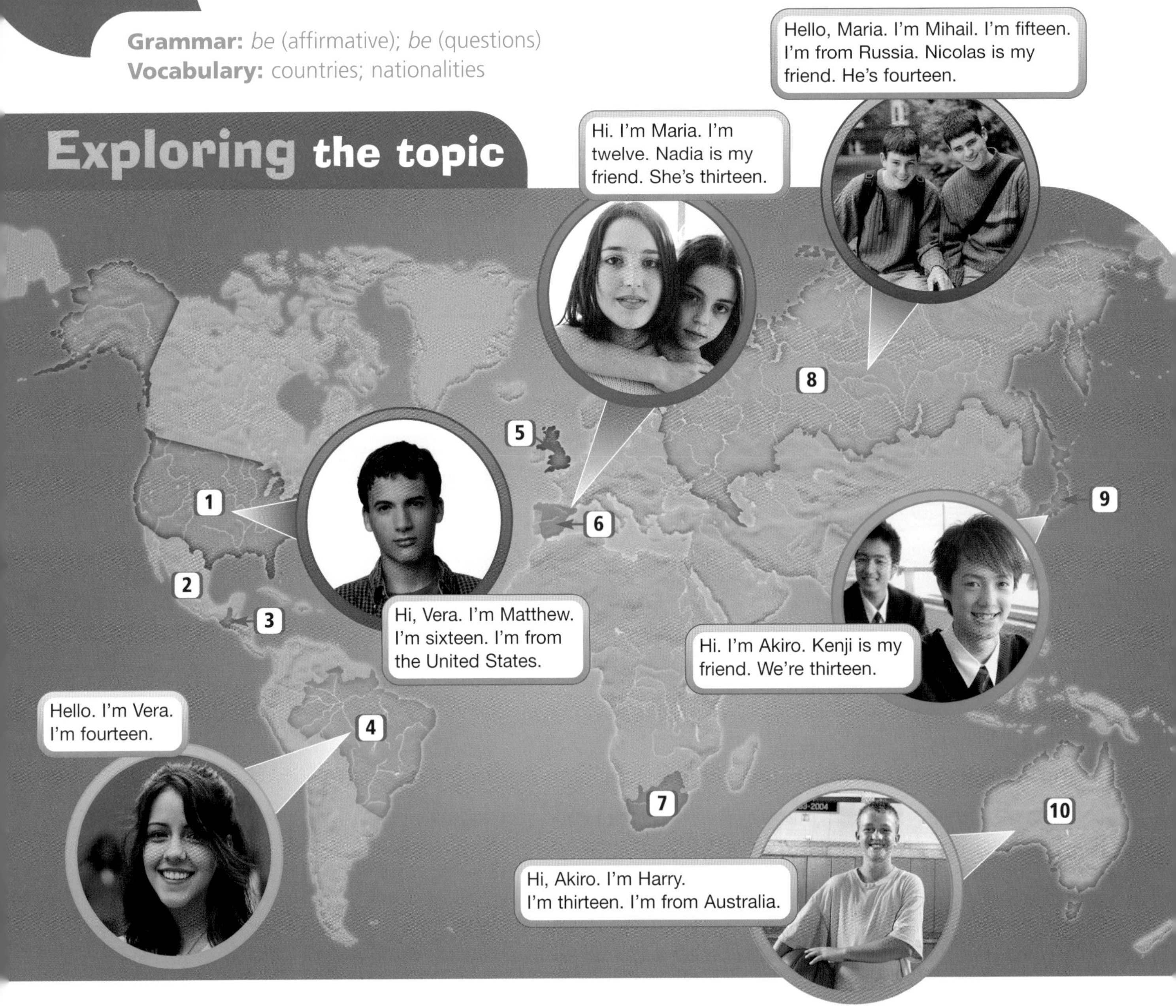

Hello, Maria. I'm Mihail. I'm fifteen. I'm from Russia. Nicolas is my friend. He's fourteen.

Hi. I'm Maria. I'm twelve. Nadia is my friend. She's thirteen.

Hi, Vera. I'm Matthew. I'm sixteen. I'm from the United States.

Hi. I'm Akiro. Kenji is my friend. We're thirteen.

Hello. I'm Vera. I'm fourteen.

Hi, Akiro. I'm Harry. I'm thirteen. I'm from Australia.

Vocabulary

1 Match the countries with the words below. Write the correct number next to the countries.

Brazil [4] the United States [ ] Spain [ ]
Russia [ ] Japan [ ] Australia [ ]
Guatemala [ ] South Africa [ ]
the United Kingdom [ ] Mexico [ ]

Now listen and repeat.

2 Read and listen to the messages.

3 Look at the map. Fill in the blanks with the words from exercise 1.

1 Vera is from ___Brazil___.
2 Maria and Nadia are from ________________.
3 Nicolas is from ________________.
4 Akiro and Kenji are from ________________.

4 Fill in the blanks.

Name: I'm ________________.
Age: I'm ________________.
Country: I'm from ________________.

Grammar

be (affirmative)

Talking about personal information

1 Look at the chart.

Affirmative	
Long form	Short form
I am Akiro.	**I'm** Akiro.
You are thirteen.	**You're** thirteen.
Nicolas is eleven. **He is** eleven.	**He's** eleven.
Vera is fourteen. **She is** fourteen.	**She's** fourteen.
Brazil is a country. **It is** a country.	**It's** a country.
We are in class.	**We're** in class.
You are from Japan.	**You're** from Japan.
Akiro and Harry are e-pals. **They are** e-pals.	**They're** e-pals.

2 Look at the picture. Match the names with the pronouns.

1	Roxy	a	he
2	Lenny and Hana	b	she
3	Mario	c	she
4	Hana	d	they

3 Fill in the blanks with *am*, *is* or *are*.

1 Roxy *is* from the United Kingdom.
2 Lenny and Bruce ______ thirteen.
3 He ______ fourteen.
4 They ______ from Australia.

4 Write the short forms.

1 He is from Guatemala. *He's* from Guatemala.
2 We are from Australia. ________ from Australia.
3 I am fifteen. ________ fifteen.
4 They are thirteen. ________ thirteen.
5 She is twelve. ________ twelve.

Finished?
Page 92, Puzzle 1A

Over to you!

5 Invent your identity and write your message.

Chat

Hi! I'm ________ (name).
I'm from ________ (country).
I'm ________ (age).
My friend is ________ (name). Bye!

Read your message to the class.

Building the topic

Vocabulary

1 **Match the nationality with the athlete.**
Write the correct number next to the countries.

10 Australian	☐ American	☐ Russian	☐ Guatemalan	☐ Mexican
☐ Brazilian	☐ Spanish	☐ Japanese	☐ British	☐ South African

Now listen and repeat.

2 **Read and listen to the interview.**
Now listen again and repeat the questions in blue.

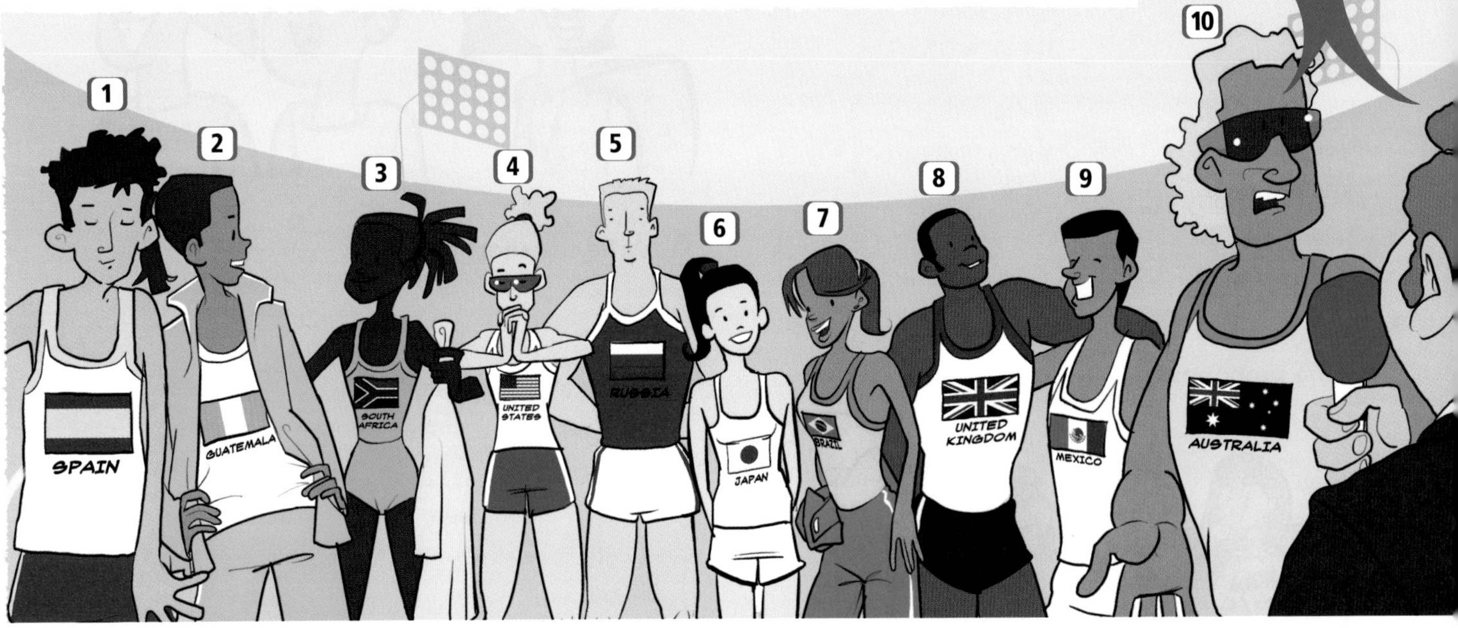

What's your name?
I'm Neil.
Where are you from?
I'm from Sydney. I'm Australian.
How old are you?
I'm 19.

1 SPAIN
2 GUATEMALA
3 SOUTH AFRICA
4 UNITED STATES
5 RUSSIA
6 JAPAN
7 BRAZIL
8 UNITED KINGDOM
9 MEXICO
10 AUSTRALIA

3 **Fill in the blanks with the country or nationality.**

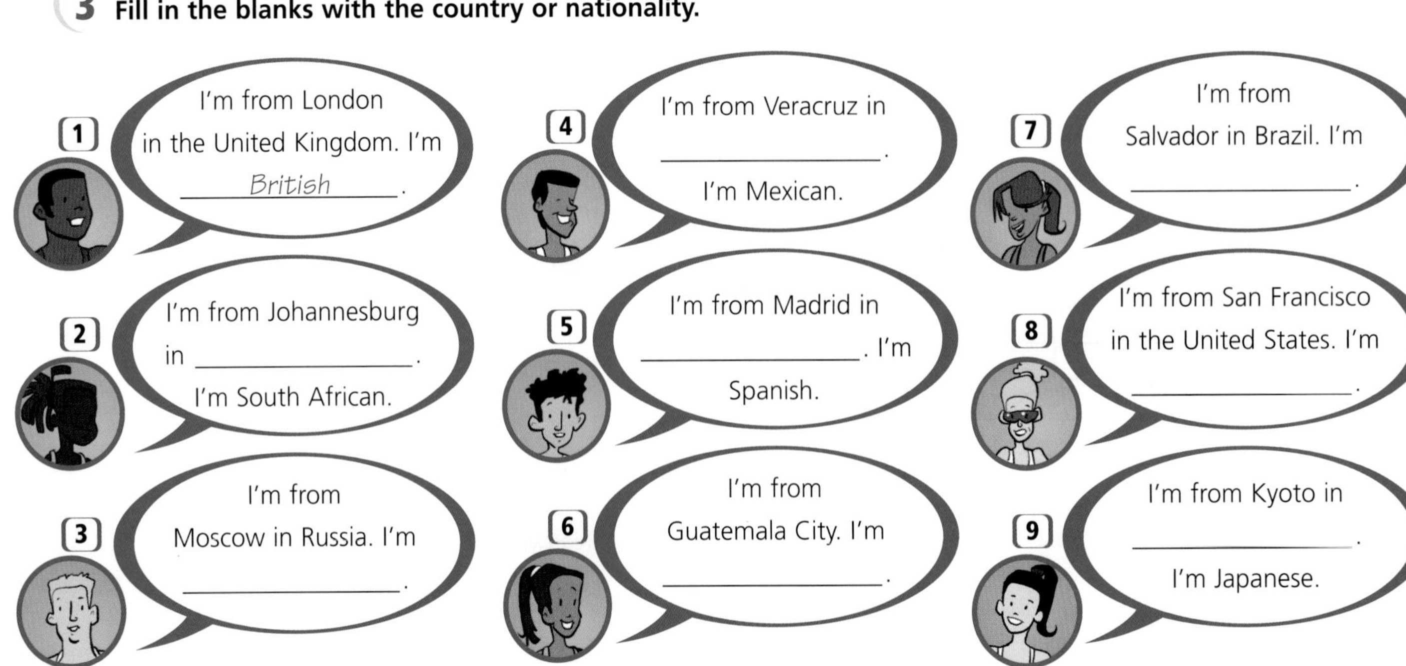

1 I'm from London in the United Kingdom. I'm British.
2 I'm from Johannesburg in ________. I'm South African.
3 I'm from Moscow in Russia. I'm ________.
4 I'm from Veracruz in ________. I'm Mexican.
5 I'm from Madrid in ________. I'm Spanish.
6 I'm from Guatemala City. I'm ________.
7 I'm from Salvador in Brazil. I'm ________.
8 I'm from San Francisco in the United States. I'm ________.
9 I'm from Kyoto in ________. I'm Japanese.

Grammar

be (questions)

Asking about personal information

1 Look at the chart.

Questions	Answers
What's your **name**?	I'm Vera. / My name's Vera.
Where are you **from**?	I'm from Brazil. / I'm Brazilian.
How old are you?	I'm 14 years old.

2 Match the questions with the answers.

1 What's your name? — a I'm twelve.
2 Where are you from? — b I'm Alex.
3 How old are you? — c I'm from South Africa.

3 Fill in the blanks with *Where*, *What* or *How old*. Complete Serena's age.

Serena Williams, September 26, 1981

1 ___What___'s your name? My name's Serena Williams.
2 __________ are you from? I'm American.
3 __________ are you? I'm ______ .

4 Fill in the blanks with the correct word.

Daniela Lima, January 12, 1984

1 ___What's___ your __________?
__________ __________'s Daniela.
2 Where __________ __________ from?
__________ from Brazil.
3 __________ __________ are you? I'm ______.

5 Fill in the blanks with the correct words.

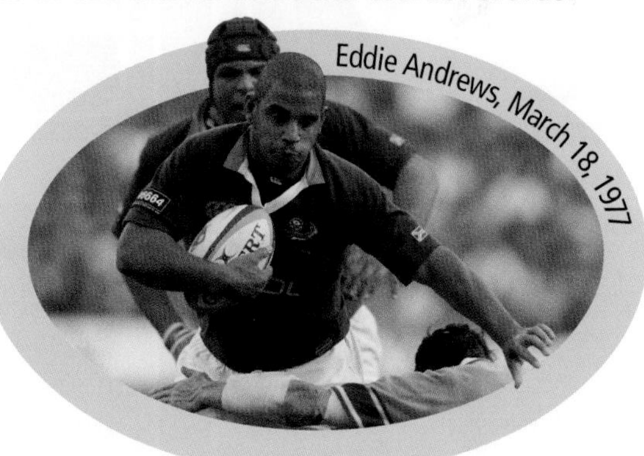

Eddie Andrews, March 18, 1977

1 ___What's___ __________ __________ ?
My __________ Eddie.
2 __________ __________ __________
__________? __________ from South Africa.
3 __________ __________ __________
__________? __________ __________ .

Finished?
Page 92, Puzzle 1B

Over to you!

6 You are a famous person. Ask and answer in class.

Student A: What's your name?
Student B: I'm Brad Pitt.
Student A: Where are you from?

Living English

Who are they?

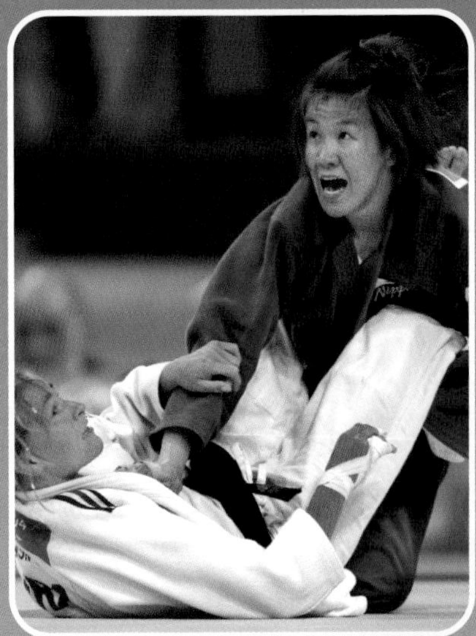

1 Tamura Ryoko

Judo player

Interviewer: What's your name?
Tamura: My name's Tamura Ryoko.
Interviewer: Where are you from?
Tamura: I'm Japanese.
Interviewer: How old are you?
Tamura: I'm thirty-three.

2

Rock violinist

Interviewer: What's your name?
Antonio: Antonio Pontarelli.
Interviewer: Where are you from?
Antonio: I'm from the United States.
Interviewer: How old are you?
Antonio: I'm seventeen.

3

Cosmonaut

Interviewer: What's your name?
Elena: My name's Elena Kondakova.
Interviewer: Where are you from?
Elena: I'm from Mitischi in Russia.
Interviewer: How old are you?
Elena: I'm thirty-seven.

Reading

1 **Look at the photos and read the text. Write the name of the person under each photo.**

2 **Read again. Circle T (True) or F (False). Correct the false sentences.**

1. Tamura is thirty-four. T / (F)
   Tamura is thirty-three.
2. Tamura is from Japan. T / F
3. Antonio is Russian. T / F
4. Antonio is twelve. T / F
5. Elena is British. T / F
6. Elena is thirty-seven. T / F

Listening

1 **Listen and circle the correct information.**

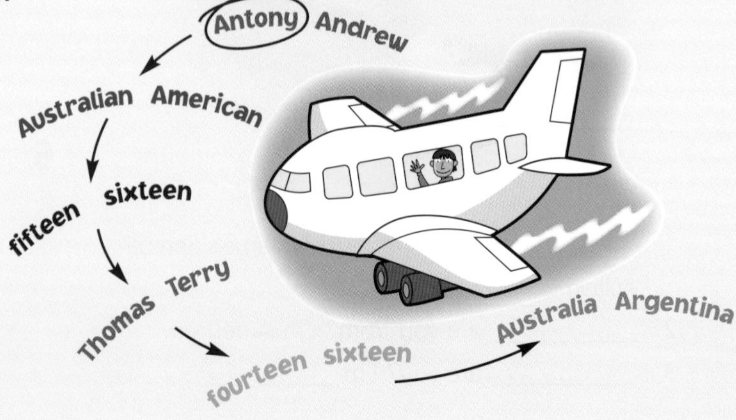

Writing

1 **Look at the Writing skills box.**

Writing skills

Subject pronouns

Always use name + verb or subject pronoun + verb.

Luke is from Australia. **He** is fifteen.

Scott and Alan are sixteen. **They** are Australian.

2 **Now read the text and circle all the subject pronouns.**

Luke is from Canberra in Australia. (He)'s Australian. He's fifteen. His friends are Scott and Alan. They're sixteen.

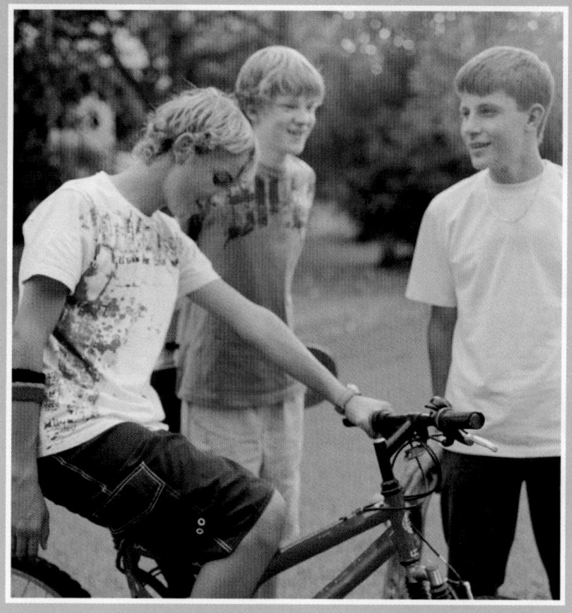

3 **Choose a person in your class / school. Fill in the chart with information about the person.**

	Example	Your person
Name	*Luke*	
Town, country	*Canberra, Australia*	
Age	*15*	
Friends	*Scott and Alan*	
Age	*16*	

4 **Now write the profile of your person. Use the text and the chart to help you.**

Speaking

1 **Listen and read.**

Hello. I'm **Brainy**. What's your name?
Hello. I'm **Electrica**. Nice to meet you.
Nice to meet you, too.

He's Virtual.
Nice to meet you, too.
Hi **Virtual**. Nice to meet you.

2 **Look at the Pronunciation box. Listen to the examples.**

Pronunciation

Contractions

We use short forms when we speak.

What's your name?

I'm Brainy.

Listen again and repeat.

3 **Listen. Circle the sentence you hear.**

1 (He's a student.) / He is a student.
2 She is Spanish. / She's Spanish.
3 You are fourteen. / You're fourteen.
4 We are from Russia. / We're from Russia.

4 **Practice the dialog with your partner.**

5 **Change the words in blue. Write a new dialog. Now practice the dialog in class.**

2 Work and play

Grammar: *be* (negative); *be* + adjective
Vocabulary: jobs; feelings

Exploring the topic

Vocabulary

1 Look at the photos. Circle the correct jobs.

1 Brad Pitt – actor / artist

2 Usher and Beyoncé – firefighters / singers

3 Daniela Lima and Abby Wambach – soccer players / teachers

4 Tony Hawk – doctor / skateboarder

5 Gisele Bündchen – model / student

2 Read the sentences about the people in the photos. Then fill in the blanks with the words below.

actor doctor firefighter artist soccer player
model singer skateboarder student teacher

Now listen and repeat.

1 He isn't an ___artist___.
He's an ___actor___.
2 They aren't ________s.
They're ________s.
3 They aren't ________s.
They're ________s.
4 He isn't a ________.
He's a ________.
5 She isn't a ________.
She's a ________.

Take note!

a / an

Singular: She is **a** singer.
He is **an** actor.
Plural: They are models.

3 Fill in the blanks with *a*, *an* or –.

1 They are ___–___ skateboarders.
2 She is ________ model.
3 We are ________ soccer players.
4 He is ________ artist.
5 Kerry and Sam are ________ fire fighters.
6 Harry is ________ actor.

Grammar

be (negative)

Talking about jobs and personal information

1 Look at the chart.

Negative					
Long form			Short form		
I	**am not**	an actor.	I	**'m not**	an actor.
You	**are not**	an artist.	You	**aren't**	an artist.
He / She / It	**is not**	a doctor.	He / She / It	**isn't**	a doctor.
We	**are not**	models.	We	**aren't**	models.
You	**are not**	singers.	You	**aren't**	singers.
They	**are not**	models.	They	**aren't**	models.

2 Circle the correct form of the negative.

1 Kevin is not / are not from Japan.
2 Sally and Paul are not / is not models.
3 Teri and I are not / is not Italian.
4 Angelo is not / are not a skateboarder.
5 You are not / is not a teacher.

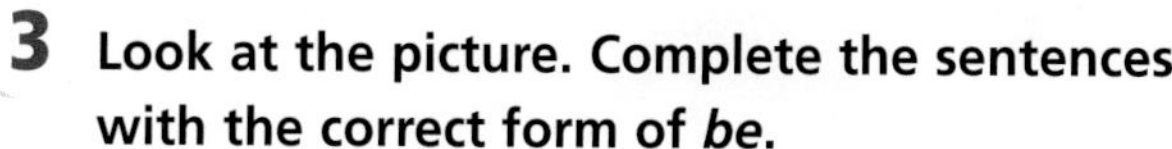

3 Look at the picture. Complete the sentences with the correct form of *be*.

1 Anna *isn't* a skateboarder.
2 Danny ____________ an artist.
3 Carl and Deb ____________ doctors.
4 Deb ____________ an actor.
5 Hong and Sue ____________ students.
6 Terry ____________ a model.

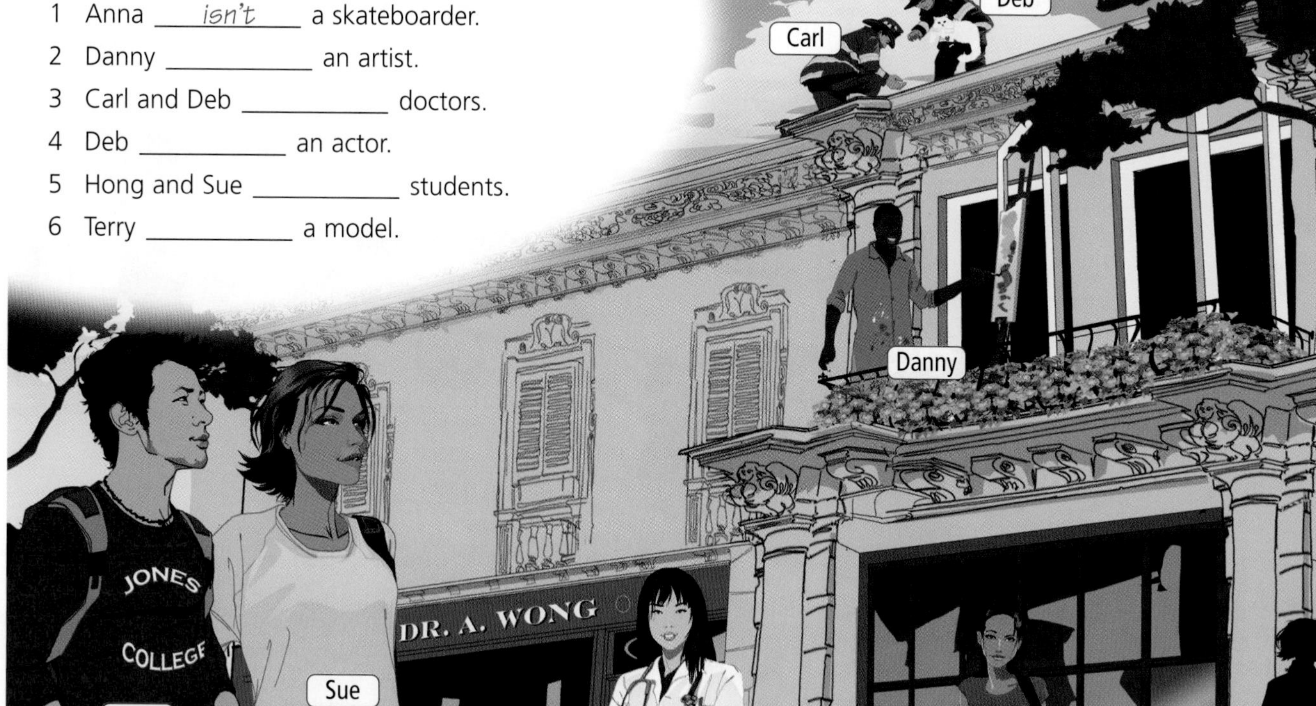

4 Make these sentences true for you.

1 I ____________ a student.
2 My teacher ____________ from Australia.
3 I ____________ in eighth grade.
4 My friends ____________ from Great Britain.
5 We ____________ in English class.
6 I ____________ Brazilian.

Finished?
Page 92, Puzzle 2A

Over to you!

5 Write 3 false sentences and one true sentence about other people. Use the affirmative. Can the class correct the false sentences?

Student A: David Beckham is an actor.
Student B: No! David Beckham isn't an actor. He's a soccer player.

Building the topic

Vocabulary

1 Look at the picture. Fill in the blanks with the words below.

tired hungry thirsty happy sad
bored angry hot cold scared

Now listen and repeat.

2 Correct the sentences about the people in the picture.

1 Pablo isn't tired. *He is hungry* .
2 Julie isn't sad. ______________.
3 Mai and Ria aren't happy. ______________.
4 Roger isn't bored. ______________.
5 Martin isn't hot. ______________.
6 Adam isn't happy. ______________.

Grammar

be + adjective

Talking about feelings

1 **Look at the chart.**

Affirmative		Negative	
I am	happy.	**I'm not**	happy.
You are	thirsty.	**You aren't**	thirsty.
He / She / It is	angry.	**He / She / It isn't**	angry.
We are	bored.	**We aren't**	bored.
You are	hungry.	**You aren't**	hungry.
They are	hot.	**They aren't**	hot.

Take note!

Adjectives never change form in English.

~~They are tireds.~~ ✗ They are tired. ✓

2 **Put the words in the correct order to make sentences.**

1 hungry / is / David *David is hungry*.
2 aren't / happy / we __________.
3 angry / are / they __________.
4 Diane / bored / isn't __________.
5 is / Roger / sad __________.
6 are / scared / Mia and Fong __________.

3 **Look at Daniel's pictures below. Fill in the blanks with the correct form of *be*.**

1 Carly and Miguel *aren't* happy.
2 Daniel and Maria ________ bored.
3 Anna, Maria and Raoul ________ hot.
4 Miguel ________ hungry.
5 Daniel and Alex ________ happy.
6 Davonda and Raoul ________ thirsty.

4 **Write one affirmative sentence and one negative sentence for the pictures below.**

1 Maria – bored / angry
Maria isn't bored.
She is angry.

2 Daniel and Alex – tired / scared
__________.
__________.

3 Anna and Miguel – happy / sad
__________.
__________.

Finished?
Page 92, Puzzle 2B

Over to you!

5 **Choose an adjective from page 16. Draw a mask. Can the class guess the adjective?**

Daniel's summer vacation with his friends

Living English

"How are you today?"

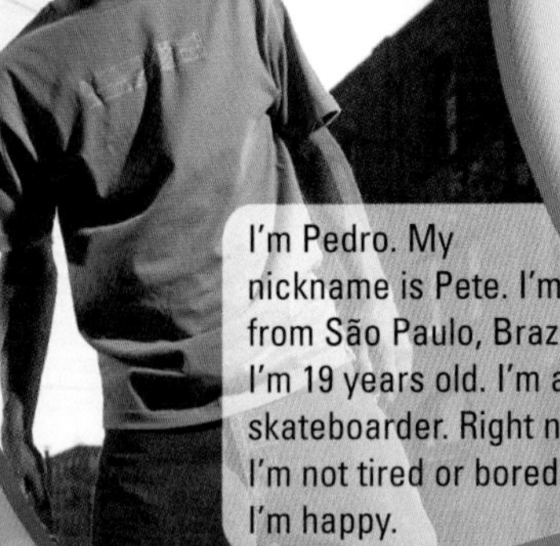

1 I'm Pedro. My nickname is Pete. I'm from São Paulo, Brazil. I'm 19 years old. I'm a skateboarder. Right now I'm not tired or bored. I'm happy.

2 I'm Edwina. My nickname is Eddie. I'm from New York City. I'm 29 years old. I'm a doctor. Right now I'm tired and hungry, but I'm not bored!

3 I'm William. My nickname is Billy. I'm from Perth, Australia. I'm 21 years old. I'm a model. Right now I'm tired and cold. I'm not happy. I'm angry!

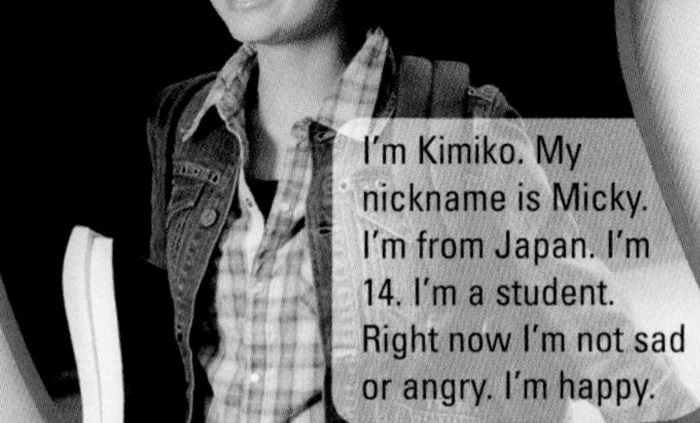

4 I'm Kimiko. My nickname is Micky. I'm from Japan. I'm 14. I'm a student. Right now I'm not sad or angry. I'm happy.

Reading

1 **Look at the Reading skills box.**

Reading skills

Using pictures

Use pictures to help you understand a text.

Now look at the photographs above. Where are the people? What are their jobs?

2 **Read the article. What is each person's real name and job?**

1 *Pedro* ______ *skateboarder* ______
2 ______ ______
3 ______ ______
4 ______ ______

3 **Read again. Circle T (True) or F (False).**

1 Pedro is from Brazil. (T) / F
2 Eddie is twenty-nine years old. T / F
3 Eddie is bored. T / F
4 William's nickname is Willy. T / F
5 Kimiko is fourteen years old. T / F
6 Kimiko is angry. T / F

Writing

1 Read the postcard. Where is Johnny? What is his friend's name?

Hi Tim!

I'm not at home! I'm in Italy. I'm with my friend, Carlo. His nickname is Carlino. He's from Rome. He's a student. Right now we're hot and tired, but we aren't bored.

See you soon!
Johnny

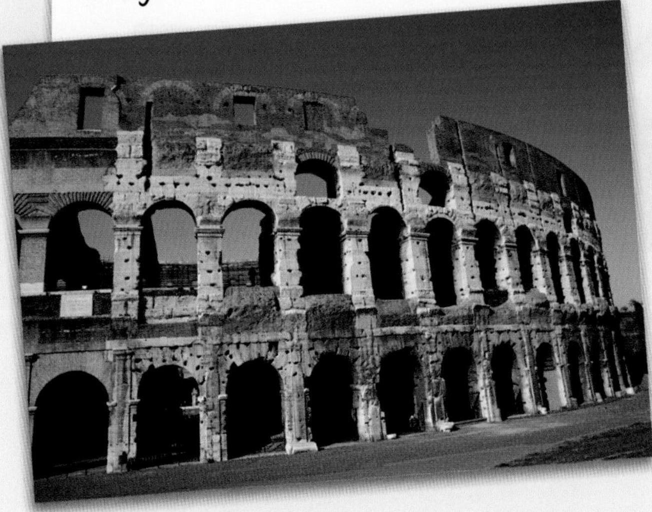

2 Fill in the chart with information about Johnny's friend.

	Johnny's friend	Your friend
Place	*Italy*	
Name	*Carlo*	
Nickname		
From		
Job		
Right now		

3 Now imagine you are in another place with a friend. Fill in the chart with your friend's information.

4 Write a postcard about your friend. Use the text and the chart to help you.

Speaking

1 Listen and read.

2 Look at the Pronunciation box. Listen to the examples.

Pronunciation

Emotions

We express emotion with our intonation.

I'm fine. I'm great. I'm hungry.

Listen again and repeat.

3 Listen. Write ↗ (up) or ↘ (down).

1 I'm ↗ happy.

2 I'm sad.

3 I'm tired.

4 I'm OK.

4 Practice the dialog with your partner.

5 Change the words in blue. Write a new dialog. Now practice the dialog in class.

Review 1

Vocabulary

Countries and nationalities

1 Fill in the blanks with the correct country or nationality.

1 Natalia is from Russia.
She's *Russian*.

2 Taro is from ________.
He's Japanese.

3 Kim is from South Africa.
She's ________.

4 Rob is from ________.
He's Australian.

5 Geri is from the United Kingdom.
She's ________.

6 Judd is from ________.
He's American.

Jobs and feelings

2 Look at the pictures. Fill in the blanks with *a* or *an* and the correct job, and the correct adjective.

1 She's *a doctor*.
She's *happy*.

2 He's ________.
He's ________.

3 He's ________.
He's ________.

4 She's ________.
She's ________.

5 She's ________.
She's ________.

6 He's ________.
He's ________.

Grammar

be (affirmative and negative)

1 Look at the photo. Fill in the blanks with the correct form of *be*. Use the affirmative and negative short forms.

Hi! I ___'m___ Nelly. I ________ from the United States. My friends ________ Fiona and Nola. They ________ American. They ________ British.

Fiona and I ________ fourteen, but Nola ________ fourteen. She ________ thirteen.

We ________ students. We ________ sad.

We ________ happy!

2 Fill in the blanks with the correct form of *be*. Use the affirmative and negative form.

1 Nelly ___is___ from the United States.
2 Fiona and Nola ________ from the United States.
3 Nelly and Fiona ________ fourteen.
4 Nelly, Fiona and Nola ________ students.
5 Nola ________ fourteen.
6 Nelly, Fiona and Nola ________ sad.

be (questions)

3 Write the questions.

You: ___What's your name___?
Nelly: My name's Nelly.
You: ________________?
Nelly: I'm fifteen.
You: ________________?
Nelly: I'm from the United States.

a / an and *be* + adjective

4 Fill in the blanks with *a*, *an* or – .

1 He's ___an___ artist.
2 They're ______ firefighters.
3 She's ______ thirsty.
4 He's ______ teacher.
5 We're ______ hungry.
6 She's ______ actor.

Study skills

Instructions

Before you do an exercise, read the instructions.

1 Match the instructions with the pictures.

1 Look — d
2 Listen
3 Repeat
4 Match
5 Read
6 Write

a (ear)
b blue— bag
c 1, 2, 3,... 1, 2, 3,...
d (eyes)
e (pen)
f (book)

2 Find examples of the instructions below in units 1 and 2. Translate into your language.

1 Fill in the blanks.
2 Match the questions with the answers.

3 Favorites

Grammar: possessive adjectives; possessive *'s*; *be* (*yes* / *no* questions)
Vocabulary: describing objects; family

Exploring the topic

Vocabulary

1 **Look at the pictures. Fill in the blanks with the words below.**

big cheap expensive long
new old short small

Now listen and repeat.

1 The skateboard is long.

2 The skateboard is ________.

3 The cell phones are ________.

4 The cell phones are ________.

5 The computer is ________.

6 The computer is ________.

7 The CD player is ________.

8 The CD player is ________.

2 **Read and listen. Then match the objects from exercise 1 with the people.**

Zoe's skateboard 1 Juan's CD player ___ Sara and Kevin's computer ___ Dana and Tami's cell phones ___

My skateboard is new and it's long. It's fantastic!

Zoe

Juan

My CD player is big, but it's cheap!

Our cell phones are small and new. They're cheap, too. They're excellent!

Dana and Tami

Sara and Kevin

Our computer is new and expensive! It's awesome.

Grammar

Possessive adjectives

Talking about possessions

1 **Look at the chart.**

Subject pronoun	Possessive adjective
I am Sara.	**My** computer is new.
You are Zoe.	**Your** skateboard is long.
He is Juan.	**His** CD player is big.
She is Dana.	**Her** phone is cheap.
It is a computer.	**Its** price is $40.
We are friends.	**Our** phones are small.
You are friends.	**Your** computer is new.
They are friends.	**Their** phones are cheap.

2 **Fill in the blanks with the correct possessive adjectives.**

My
pen is expensive.
1
Ricky

______ notebook is small.
2
Nelly

______ pencils are short.
Leon
3
Joe

______ eraser is big.
Hector
4

______ ruler is big.
5
Jen
Gena

______ bag is old.
6
Adam

Possessive *'s*

Talking about possessions

3 **Look at the chart.**

Possessive *'s*

She is Zoe. Her skateboard is long.
Zoe's skateboard is long.

He is Juan. His CD player is big.
Juan's CD player is big.

4 **Look at the pictures in exercise 2. Fill in the blanks.**

1 ___Ricky's___ pen is expensive.
2 ______________ notebook is small.
3 Leon and ______________ pencils are short.
4 ______________ eraser is big.
5 Jen and ______________ ruler is long.
6 ______________ bag is old.

Finished?
Page 93, Puzzle 3A

Over to you!

5 **Describe an object in the classroom. Can the class guess the object?**

Student A: It's small and new.
Student B: It's a book!

Building the topic

Vocabulary

1 Fill in the blanks in the family tree with the words below.

father sister brother grandmother
grandfather grandparents mother parents

Now listen and repeat.

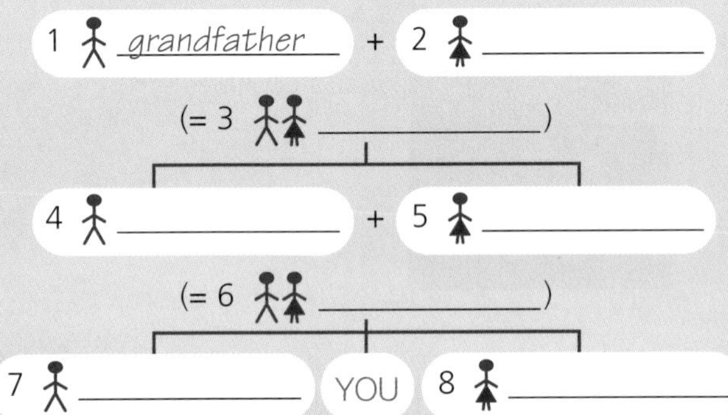

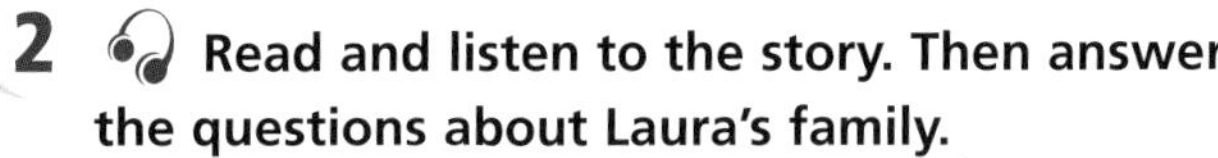

2 Read and listen to the story. Then answer the questions about Laura's family.

1 Who is a musician? *Her mother*.
2 Who is 85? ____.
3 Who are five? ____.
4 Who is a skateboarder? ____.
5 Who is Kath? ____.
6 Who is Dave? ____.

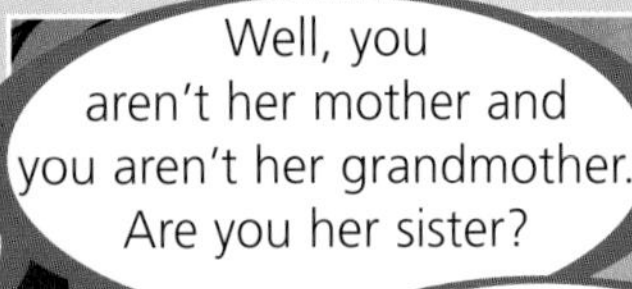

Grammar

be (*yes* / *no* questions)

Asking and answering about people and things

1 **Look at the chart.**

Question	Short answers
Am I right?	Yes, **I am**. / No, **I'm not**.
Are you Dave?	Yes, **you are**. / No, **you aren't**.
Is he your father?	Yes, **he is**. / No, **he isn't**.
Is she your mother?	Yes, **she is**. / No, **she isn't**.
Is it your house?	Yes, **it is**. / No, **it isn't**.
Are we friends?	Yes, **we are**. / No, **we aren't**.
Are you brothers?	Yes, **you are**. / No, **you aren't**.
Are they five?	Yes, **they are**. / No, **they aren't**.

2 **Complete the questions about Laura's family.**

1 *Are* you Laura's mother?

2 ______ he Laura's father?

3 ______ ______ her mother?

4 ______ they her brothers?

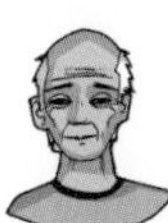

5 ______ ______ her father?

6 ______ ______ her grandmother?

3 **Match the answers with the questions in exercise 2.**

a No, he isn't. ______
b No, she isn't. ______
c Yes, they are. ______
d Yes, he is. ______
e Yes, she is. ______
f No, I'm not. *1*

4 **Look at the pictures. Write short answers for the questions.**

1 

2 

3 

4 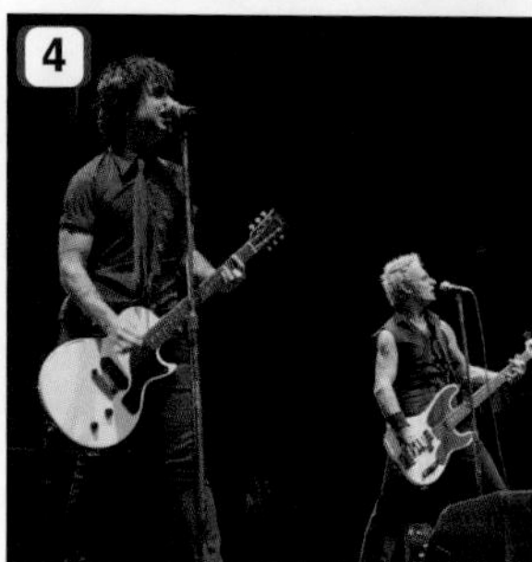

5 

6 

1 Are you a skateboarder? *No, I'm not*.
2 Is he an actor? ______________.
3 Are they soccer players? ______________.
4 Are we singers? ______________.
5 Is she Beyoncé? ______________.
6 Are you a student? ______________.

Finished?
Page 93, Puzzle 3B

Over to you!

5 **Write the names of four people in your family. Ask and answer in class.**

Student A: Is Marco your brother?
Student B: No, he isn't.
Student A: Is he your father?
Student B: Yes, he is.

Living English

Famous People Quiz

Britney Spears is a popular singer. Her sister's name is Jamie Lynn Spears. What is Jamie Lynn?

a a singer   b an athlete   c an actor

Venus Williams is a famous tennis player. Her sister is too. What is her name?

a Alicia   b Mary   c Serena

Avril Lavigne is a young singer. She is from Canada. What is the name of her hometown?

a Napanee   b Toronto   c Vancouver

Keane is a famous band. What nationality are they?

a British   b Canadian   c American

Tom Welling is the star of the TV program Smallville. What is his brother Mark Welling?

a a singer   b an artist   c an actor

Natalie Imbruglia is a singer. Where is she from?

a America   b Britain   c Australia

Reading

1 Look at the Reading skills box.

Reading skills

Predicting

You can predict vocabulary in a text before you read.

Now look at the names in the text. Write what you know about the people.

Britney Spears, singer, American?

2 Read the quiz. Mark your answers. Check your answers at the bottom of the page.

3 Read again. Write the names.

1 Her hometown is in Canada. *Avril Lavigne*
2 His brother is an actor. ____________
3 They are British. ____________
4 They are tennis players. ____________ and ____________
5 She's Australian. ____________

Answers 1c 2c 3a 4a 5c 6c

Listening

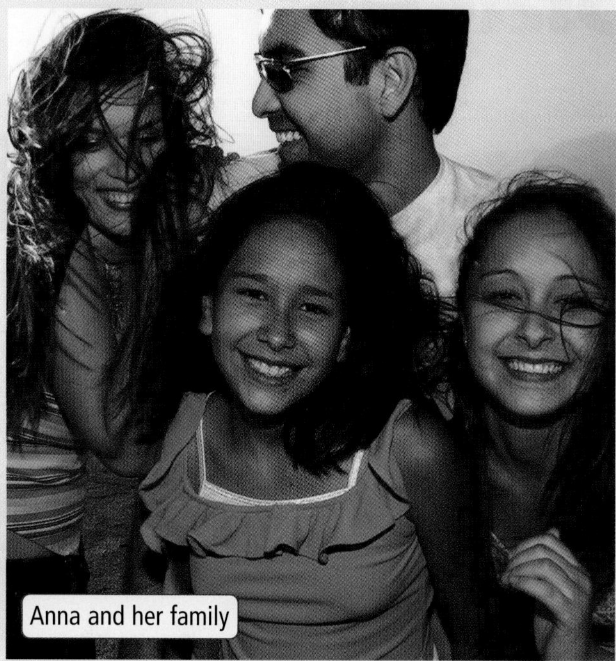
Anna and her family

1 **Look at the photos and listen to the conversation. Answer the questions about Anna.**

1 What's her job? *Tennis player*
2 How old is she? ______
3 Where is she from? ______

2 **Listen again. Fill in the chart about Anna's family. Use the words below.**

firefighter David Maria soccer player
tennis player Helena

	Name	Job
father	*David*	
mother		
sister		

Writing

1 **Read the e-mail. Who is Megan? Who is Holly?**

From: Chris
To: Ashley
Subject: my cool family

Hi Ashley
My family is cool! My father is a firefighter. His name is Andrew. My mom's name is Megan and she's an artist. My sister's name is Holly and she's eighteen. She's a student. My other sister's name is Emily. She's twenty-two and she's a singer.
What about your family?
Write soon,
Chris

2 **Fill in the chart with information about Chris's family.**

	Name	Age	Job
Chris's father	*Andrew*	*X*	*firefighter*
Chris's mother		*X*	
Chris's sisters			
my ______			
my ______			
my ______			
my ______			

3 **Now fill in the chart with information about your family.**

4 **Write an e-mail about your family. Use the text and the chart to help you.**

4 Special places

Grammar: *there is / there are*; prepositions of place
Vocabulary: nature; places in a town

Exploring the topic

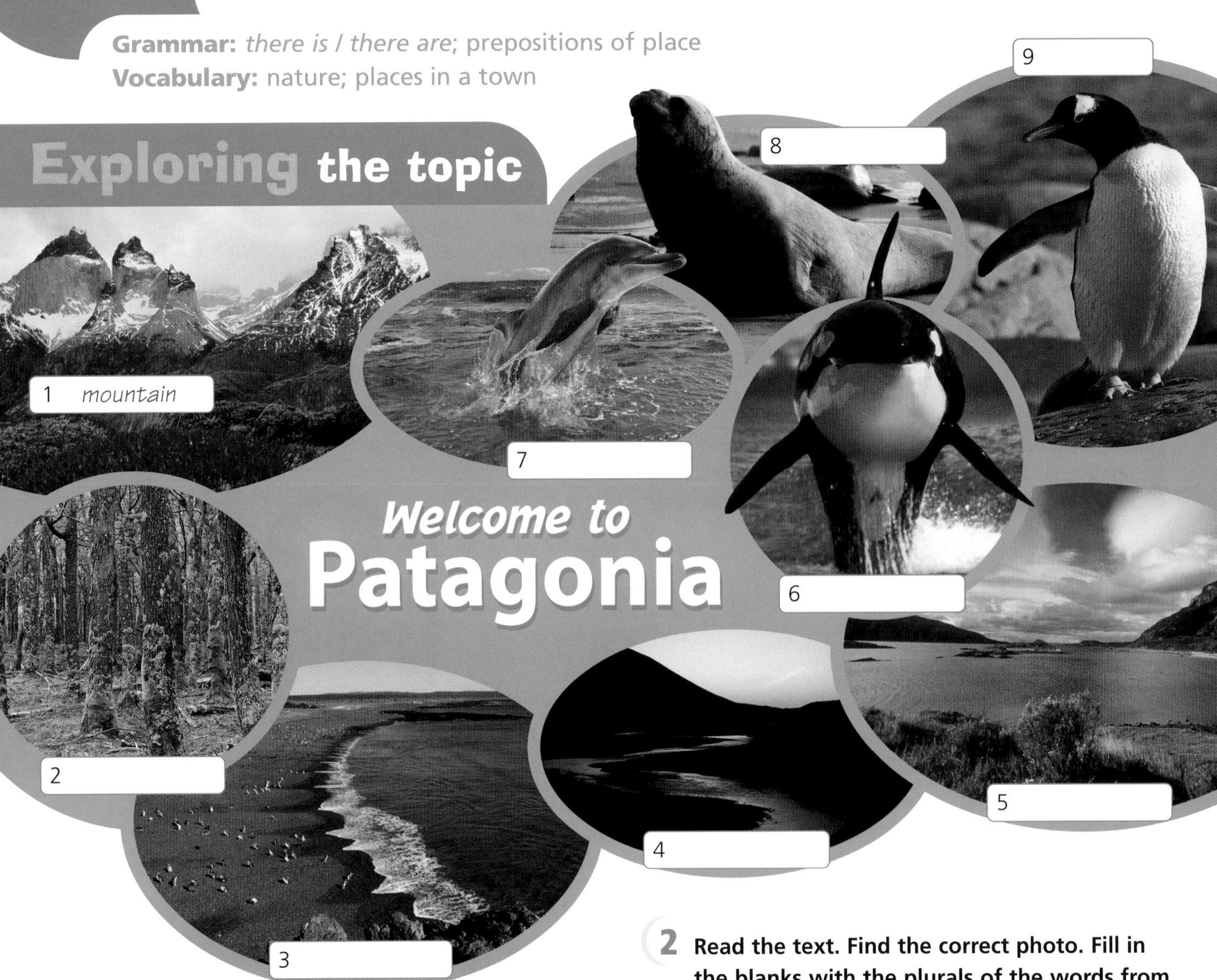

Vocabulary

1 Label the photos with the words below.

Places: mountain lake forest river beach
Animals: seal penguin whale dolphin

Now listen and repeat.

Take note!

Plural nouns

a seal seal**s**
a beach beach**es**

2 Read the text. Find the correct photo. Fill in the blanks with the plurals of the words from the photos.

There is a beautiful area in South America. Its name is Patagonia. Patagonia is very big! There are big (1) *mountains*, green (2) *f*______, beautiful (3) *b*______, long (4) *r*______, and (5) *l*______. There are beautiful animals in Patagonia. For example, there are (6) *w*______, (7) *d*______ and (8) *s*______.

- Is there a big city in Patagonia?
  Yes, there is.
- Are there any (9) *p*______?
  Yes, there are!

Now listen and check.

Grammar

there is / there are

Talking about what exists in a place

1 Look at the chart.

Affirmative	
Singular	Plural
There is a city.	**There are** mountains.
There's a river.	**There are** three rivers.

2 Look at the picture of the park. Fill in the blanks with *There is* or *There are.*

1 *There are* two tigers.
2 ______________ a panda.
3 ______________ two dolphins.
4 ______________ a whale.
5 ______________ three penguins.
6 ______________ a bear.

3 Look at the chart.

Questions and short answers	
Singular	Plural
Is there a city in Patagonia?	**Are there** any penguins?
Yes, **there is**.	Yes, **there are**.
No, **there isn't**.	No, **there aren't**.

4 Complete the questions and answers about the park.

A: Are there any penguins?
B: Yes, there (1) *are*.

A: Are there any tigers?
B: Yes, there (2) ________.

A: Is there a panda?
B: Yes, (3) ________ ________.

A: ________ ________ any seals?
B: No, (4) ________ ________.

A: ________ ________ a whale?
B: Yes, (5) ________ ________.

A: ________ ________ a bear?
B: Yes, (6) ________ ________.

Finished?
Page 95, Puzzle 4A

Over to you!

5 Think of a special place. Write 3 sentences about the place. Use words from page 28.

There is a mountain.
There are dolphins.

Now tell the class. Can they guess the special place?

Building the topic

Vocabulary

1 **Match the photos with the words. Write the correct letter next to the words.**

C	cyber café		music store
	fast food restaurant		clothes store
	sports store		bus stop
	movie theater		restrooms

Now listen and repeat.

Shopping Mall

A 

B 

C 

D 

E 

F 

G 

H 

2 **Listen. Where are the people? Write the correct number in the box.**

	fast food restuarant				restrooms
1	bus stop		cyber café		movie theater

3 **Read the text. Fill in the blanks with the correct words.**

Now listen and check.

My Ideal Shopping Mall

Jake, 13

The (1) _movie theater_ is next to the cyber café.

The (2) ______________ is between the movie theater and the fast food restaurant.

The restrooms are next to the (3) ______________.

The (4) ______________ is across from the movie theater.

The clothes store is between the sports store and the (5) ______________.

The (6) ______________ is in front of the shopping mall.

Grammar

Prepositions of place

Talking about position

1 **Look at the chart.**

Questions and answers	
Where is the sports store? It's **across from** the movie theater.	?
Where is the fast food restaurant? It's **next to** the restrooms.	?
Where is the cyber café? It's **between** the movie theater and the fast food restaurant.	?
Where is the bus stop? It's **in front of** the shopping mall.	?

2 **Look at the picture of Busy Street below. Write complete sentences.**

1 music store / cyber café
The music store is *next to* the cyber café.

2 bus stop / cyber café
The bus stop is ______________ the cyber café.

3 sports store / music store
The sports store ______________________________.

4 movie theater / music store
The ______________________________________.

5 sports store / fast food restaurant / clothes store
The ______________________________________.

3 **Where are these people? Find them in the picture and answer the questions.**

1 Where is Kathy?
Kathy is next to the cyber café.

2 Where are Liz and Ronaldo?
______________________________________.

3 Where is Akiro?
______________________________________.

4 Where is Clive?
______________________________________.

5 Where is Maria?
______________________________________.

6 Where are Sasha and Javier?
______________________________________.

Finished?
Page 95, Puzzle 4B

Over to you!

4 **Draw your ideal shopping mall. Ask and answer in class.**

Student A: Where is the cyber café?
Student B: It's next to the sports store.

Living English

Welcome to MANHATTAN – the center of New York!

Shopping

Macy's is a very big store. It's between Broadway and Seventh Avenue. It's 150 years old. There are one million different things in the store!

Famous Buildings

There are about 200 tall buildings in Manhattan. The Empire State Building is on Fifth Avenue. It's 75 years old, and it's VERY tall! It's 443 meters tall!

Central Park

Central Park is in Manhattan, too. It isn't a small park. It's 4 kilometers long. The MET (the Metropolitan Museum Of Art) is in the park.

Sports

Madison Square Garden is a sports arena. It is the home of the New York Knicks basketball team. There is a women's basketball team, too – New York Liberty. There are 20,000 seats in the arena.

Reading

1 Look at the photos and the text. Is the text about:

1 London? 2 New York? 3 Tokyo?

2 Match the attractions with the numbers.

1 The Empire State Building — D
2 Macy's
3 Central Park
4 Madison Square Garden

A one million
B four kilometers
C twenty thousand
D four hundred forty-three

3 Answer the following questions.

1 What tall building is on Fifth Avenue?
The Empire State Building.
2 How old is the Empire State Building?
3 What is Madison Square Garden?
4 What are the names of two basketball teams?
5 Where is the MET?
6 How old is Macy's department store?

Writing

1 Look at the Writing skills box.

Writing skills

Capital letters
Countries (**B**razil)
Cities (**N**ew **Y**ork)
Names of places (**C**entral **P**ark)
Monuments (**E**mpire **S**tate **B**uilding)

2 Now read the text and circle four examples of capital letters.

London is a special place in England. Buckingham Palace, Big Ben and Tower Bridge are famous buildings.

There is a big stadium. It's called Wembley. There is a big park, too. It's called Hyde Park. London is cool and fun.

3 Put capital letters in the sentences.

1 I'm from germany.
2 The eiffel tower in paris is very tall.

4 Choose a special place and fill in the chart.

	Example	Your place
City	*London*	
Country	*England*	
Famous buildings	*Buckingham Palace* *Big Ben* *Tower Bridge*	
Place 1 Name	*stadium* *Wembley*	
Place 2 Name	*park* *Hyde Park*	
Description	*cool, fun*	

5 Write a description of your place. Use the text and the chart to help you.

Speaking

1 Listen and read.

2 Look at the Pronunciation box. Listen to the examples.

Pronunciation

'o' sounds
There are two different 'o' sounds.

/a/	/ɔ/
stop	store

Listen again and repeat.

3 Listen. Put the words in the correct column.

sports dolphin forest your from short

/a/	/ɔ/
	sports

4 Practice the dialog with your partner.

5 Change the words in blue. Write a new dialog. Now practice the dialog in class.

Review 2

Vocabulary

Describing objects

1 Fill in the blanks with the words below.

big cheap expensive long
new old short small

1 Your skateboard is _long_. My skateboard is _short_!

2 The dog isn't __________. It's __________!

3 The car isn't __________. It's very __________!

4 It isn't __________. It's __________. But it's very good!

Family

2 This is Daniela's family tree. Fill in the blanks with the words below.

father brother grandfather
grandmother mother sister

(1) _grandfather_ Alberto + Angelina (2) __________

(3) __________ Pedro + Teresa (4) __________

(5) __________ David Daniela Anna (6) __________

Nature

3 Write A (Animal) or P (Place) next to the words.

1 seal _A_ 2 mountain ___ 3 dolphin ___
4 penguin ___ 5 whale ___ 6 forest ___

Places in a town

4 Label the pictures with the names of places in a town.

1 _cyber café_
2 __________
3 __________
4 __________
5 __________
6 __________
7 __________
8 __________

Grammar

Possessive adjectives

1 Fill in the blanks with *my, your, his, her, our* or *their*.

1 _My_ name is Tomiko and **I'm** from Japan.
2 This is my friend **David**. ________ father is a firefighter.
3 "What's ________ name?" "My name's Max."
4 **Susie** and ________ sister are students.
5 **Pavel and Lydia** are Americans, but ________ mother and father are from Russia.
6 **We** are twelve. ________ friend is thirteen.

Possessive *'s*

2 Write complete sentences.

1 Erica / Lara / mother
Erica is Lara's mother.
2 Ricardo and Erica / Lara / parents
______________________.
3 Henri / Lara / brother
______________________.
4 Helena and Lara / Henri / sisters
______________________.
5 Ricardo / Lara / father
______________________.

be (*yes* / *no* questions)

3 Complete the questions.

1 *Are you* from Mexico? Yes, I am.
2 ________ seventeen? No, she isn't.
3 ________ happy? Yes, they are.
4 ________ your mother? Yes, she is.
5 ________ Japanese? No, I'm not.

there is / *there are*

4 Look at the picture. Complete the questions and the answers.

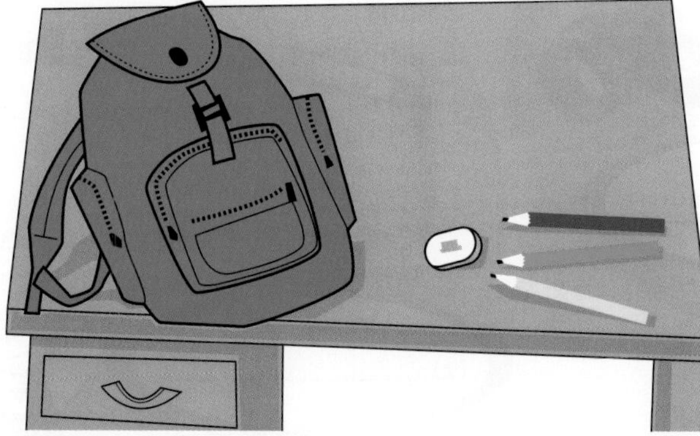

1 *Is* *there* a bag? Yes, *there* *is*.
2 ______ ______ a notebook? ______, ______ ______.
3 ______ ______ an eraser? ______, ______ ______.
4 ______ ______ ______ pencils? ______, ______ ______.
5 ______ ______ ______ pens? ______, ______ ______.

Prepositions of place

5 Look at the picture. Fill in the blanks with the correct preposition.

1 The movie theater is *across from* the shopping mall.
2 The cyber café is ________ the movie theater and the music store.
3 The sports store is ________ the music store.
4 The bus stop is ________ the music store.
5 Amy and her friends are ________ the cyber café.

Study skills

Vocabulary

In your notebook, make a vocabulary section for new words. Use pictures, translations, and example sentences.

1 Look at these notes. Which word is it?

2 Add the words to your notebook. For each word:
- **draw a picture**
- **write an example sentence**
- **write a translation**

seal lake bus stop grandfather expensive

5 Cool things

Grammar: *this / that / these / those*; plural nouns
Vocabulary: objects; furniture

Exploring the topic

Vocabulary

1 Look at the photos. Fill in the blanks with the words below.

calculators cameras telephones radios
television game console stereo CD player

Now listen and repeat.

2 Write S (singular) or P (plural).

1 Calculators P
2 game console ___
3 stereo ___
4 cameras ___
5 radios ___

This is a (1) television.

That is a (2)________________.

These are (3)________________.

Those are (4)________________.

Those are (7)________________.

That is a (8)________________.

This is a (5)________________.

These are (6)________________.

Grammar

this / that / these / those

this / these – talking about things near to us

that / those – talking about things not near to us

1 Look at the chart.

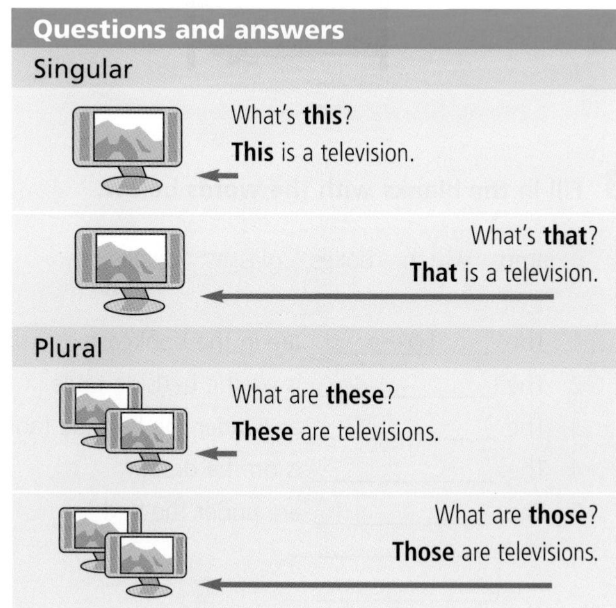

Questions and answers

Singular

What's **this**?
This is a television.

What's **that**?
That is a television.

Plural

What are **these**?
These are televisions.

What are **those**?
Those are televisions.

2 Circle the correct word.

1 (This) / These is my video game.
2 That / Those are my DVDs.
3 These / This are our radios.
4 That / Those is Tia's computer.
5 That / Those are my favorite CDs.

3 Complete the sentences with *This*, *That*, *These*, or *Those*.

1 ___*This*___ is my cell phone.

2 __________ is my game console.

3 __________ are our MP3 players.

4 __________ are my CDs.

4 Read the dialog. Then complete the questions.

Boy: What (1) ___*'s this*___ ?
Girl: This is my CD player.
Boy: What (2) __________ ?
Girl: Those are my books.
Boy: What (3) __________ ?
Girl: That is my TV.
Boy: What (4) __________ ?
Girl: These are my favorite magazines.
Boy: What (5) __________ ?
Girl: This is my new CD.
Boy: Wow! (6) __________ your room?
Girl: Yes, this is my room!

Finished?
Page 95, Puzzle 5A

Over to you!

5 Ask and answer about objects in the classroom.

Student A: What's this?
Student B: This is a notebook.
Student A: What are those?

Building the topic

Vocabulary

1 **Look at the picture. Label the objects and furniture with the words below.**

Objects: box glass dish lamp poster watch

Furniture: bed bookcase desk closet bedside table chair

Now listen and repeat.

2 **What other objects can you see in the picture? Tell the class.**

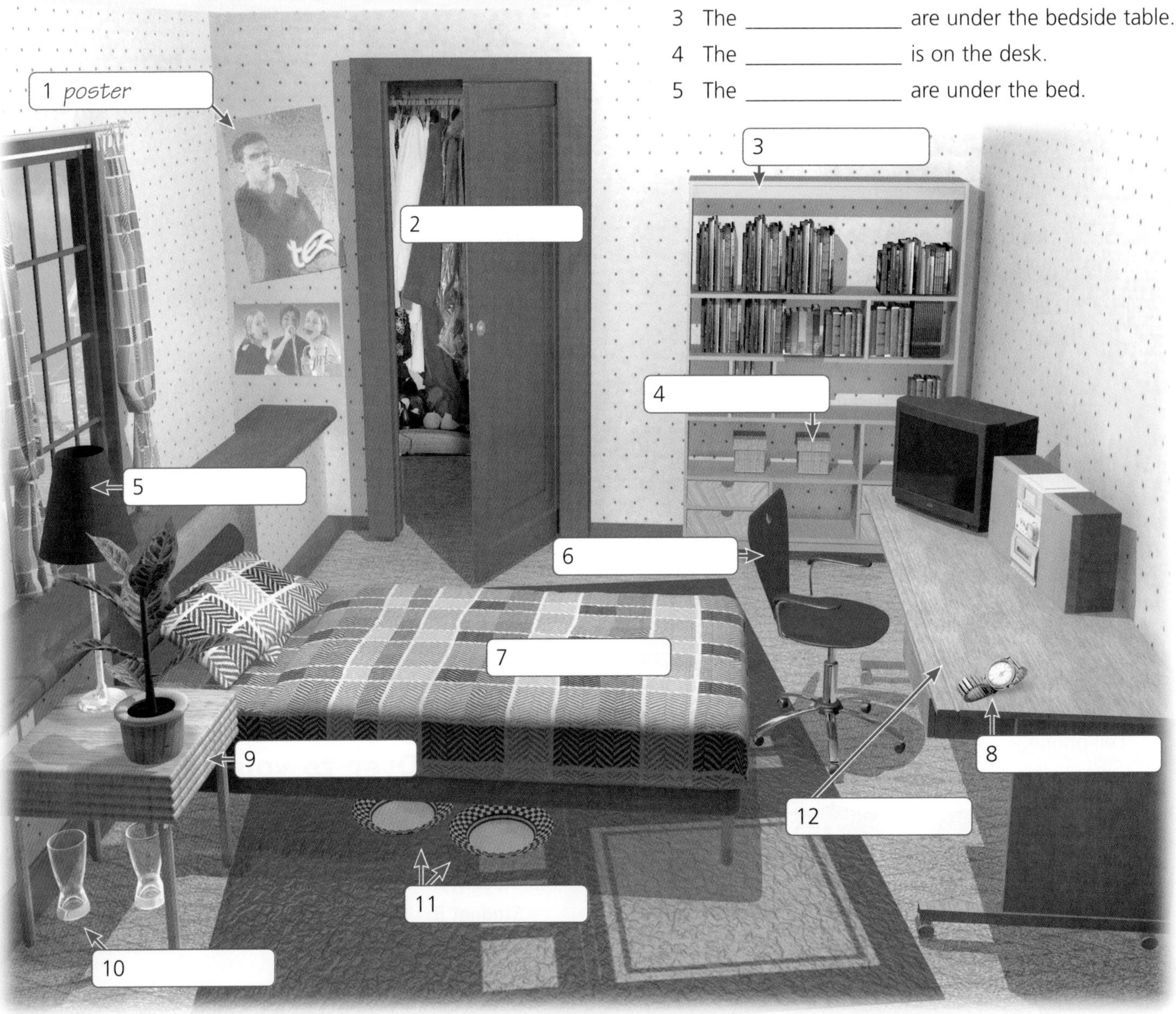

Take note!

Prepositions

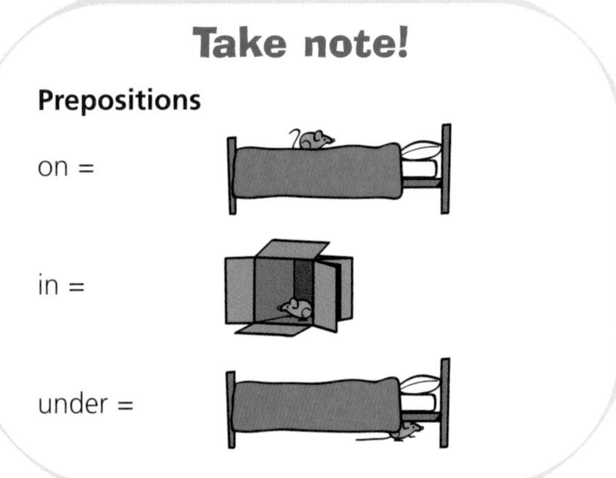
on =

in =

under =

3 **Fill in the blanks with the words below.**

lamp watch boxes glasses dishes

1 The *boxes* are in the bookcase.
2 The ______________ is on the bedside table.
3 The ______________ are under the bedside table.
4 The ______________ is on the desk.
5 The ______________ are under the bed.

1 *poster*
2
3
4
5
6
7
8
9
10
11
12

Grammar

Plural nouns

Talking about two or more things or people

1 Look at the chart.

Singular	Plural
add *-s*	
one poster	two poster**s**
one lamp	three lamp**s**
add *-es* after *-x*, *-sh*, *-ss*, and *-ch*	
one box	two box**es**
one dish	three dish**es**
one glass	four glass**es**
one watch	five watch**es**

2 Write the plurals of the words below.

Singular	Plural
bed	*beds*
book	
cell phone	
dish	
magazine	
CD	
watch	
television	
camera	

3 Look at the pictures. Write the correct number and the plural.

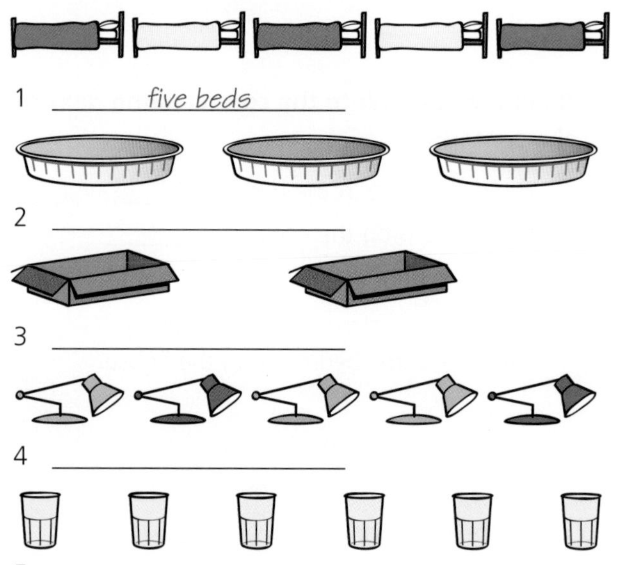

1 *five beds*

2 ______

3 ______

4 ______

5 ______

4 Find the objects in the picture. How many are there? Write sentences.

1 *There are nine books*. (book)
2 ______. (glass)
3 ______. (poster)
4 ______. (CD)
5 ______. (watch)
6 ______. (box)

Finished?
Page 95, Puzzle 5B

Over to you!

5 Write down the things in your classroom. How many are there?

There are thirty desks. There is one door.

Compare with the class. Who is correct?

Living English

Is it a house? No, it's a …

Is it a house? Is it a boat?
Well, it's two things – it's a houseboat. It's on the Columbia River in Oregon, U.S. In my houseboat, there are two rooms – a living room and a bedroom. There are lots of cool things in the living room: a big TV, a DVD player, and a bed! There are eight windows and two doors. The bedroom is very small. There are two beds and a radio. My houseboat is small, but it's very cool because it's on the river. And it's a boat, so it isn't always in the same place!

David, Oregon

My house is a cave! It's in the mountains near Granada, Spain. In my house there is a living room, a kitchen, three bedrooms and a bathroom. My bedroom is big. There's a bed, a desk and a bookcase, and there are two chairs. There is a TV, but there isn't a DVD player. There's a door, of course, but there isn't a window! There are only three windows in the house! Sometimes there is Flamenco dancing in our living room. Our house is really different. It's great!
Mariana, Spain

Reading

1 Look at the Reading skills box.

Reading skills

Text types

Texts can be from different places, for example books, magazines, newspapers, or the Internet.

Now read the text. Is it:

1 an e-mail?
2 a magazine article?
3 an advertisement?

2 Read the text. Write the correct name next to the sentences.

1 There is a radio in the bedroom. *David*
2 The house is on the river. ___________
3 There are only three windows in the house. ___________
4 There are three bedrooms in the house. ___________
5 There is a bed in the living room. ___________
6 The house is in the mountains. ___________
7 The bedroom isn't big. ___________
8 There isn't a DVD player. ___________

Listening

1 **Listen. Write the number of the advertisements under the photos.**

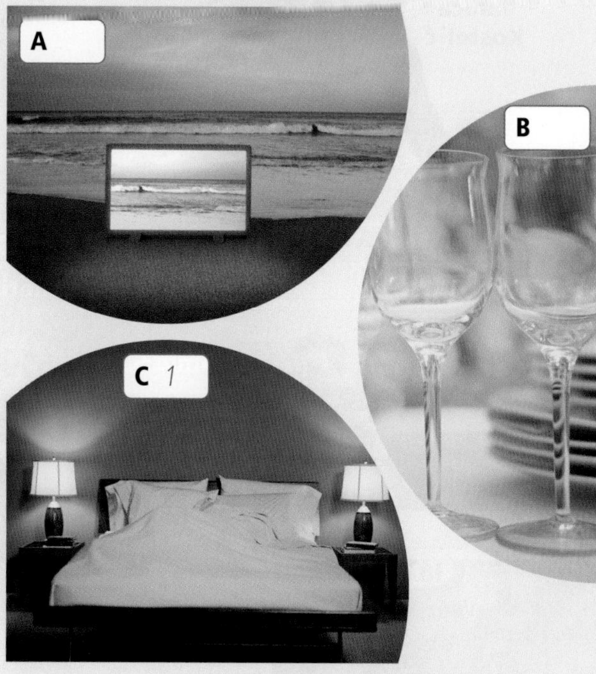

Take note!

Prices
$40 = forty dollars
$220 = two hundred twenty dollars

2 **Listen again. Check (✓) the items you hear for each store and fill in the missing prices.**

	Bedroom Bonanza	Electric City	Super Stores
beds	✓		
bedside tables			
cameras			
CD players			
cell phones			
chairs			
computers			
desks			
dishes			
glasses			
posters			
televisions			
Prices	$40 – $200	$ __ – $220	$10 – ____

Writing

1 **Read the text. Draw the missing objects in the plan.**

Lisa's bedroom

This is my bedroom. It's my favorite room in the house. There is a bed, a closet, a desk and a bedside table. There is a lamp on the bedside table. There is a television on the desk. There are two plants on the desk, too. There are posters on the wall.

2 **Fill in the chart with information about Lisa's bedroom.**

Lisa's bedroom	My bedroom
a bed	

3 **Now fill in the chart with information about your bedroom.**

4 **Write about your bedroom. Use the text and the chart to help you.**

6 Fun and games

Grammar: *can*; imperatives
Vocabulary: abilities; sports rules

Exploring the topic

Vocabulary

1 **Look at the photos. Fill in the blanks with the words below.**

dance swim ice-skate ski jump high
run fast ride a horse play basketball

Now listen and repeat.

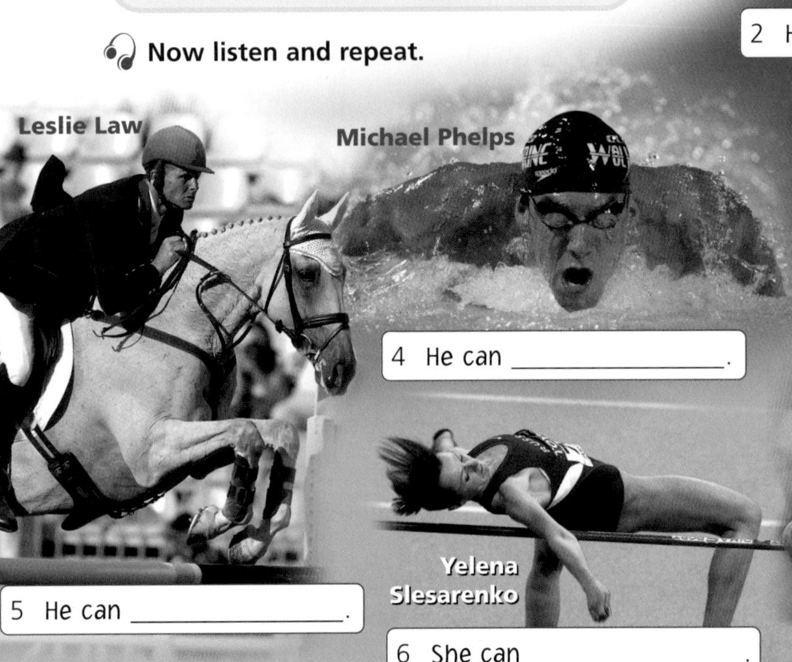

2 **Read and listen to the questions. Then check ✓ (*Yes, I can*) or ✗ (*No, I can't*).**

	Yes, I can. (✓)	No, I can't. (✗)
Can you swim?	☐	☐
Can you dance?	☐	☐
Can you ice-skate?	☐	☐
Can you jump high?	☐	☐
Can you play basketball?	☐	☐
Can you ski?	☐	☐
Can you run fast?	☐	☐
Can you ride a horse?	☐	☐

3 **Choose two activities you can do, and two activities you can't do. Fill in the blanks with the verb.**

1 I can ________________________________.
2 I can ________________________________.
3 I can't ________________________________.
4 I can't ________________________________.

Grammar

can

Talking about ability

1 Look at the chart.

Affirmative		Negative	
I	**can** swim.	I	**can't** swim.
You	**can** dance.	You	**can't** dance.
He / She / It	**can** run fast.	He / She / It	**can't** run fast.
We	**can** ice-skate.	We	**can't** ice-skate.
You	**can** jump high.	You	**can't** jump high.
They	**can** ski.	They	**can't** ski.

2 Look at the pictures. Write sentences.

1 He can't ___ski___.
2 She can ______.
3 They ______.
4 ______.
5 ______.
6 ______.

3 Look at the chart.

Questions and short answers			
Can	I	swim?	Yes, I **can**. / No, I **can't**.
Can	you	run fast?	Yes, you **can**. / No, you **can't**.
Can	he / she / it	dance?	Yes, he / she / it **can**. / No, he / she / it **can't**.
Can	we	sing?	Yes, we **can**. / No, we **can't**.
Can	you	ice-skate?	Yes, you **can**. / No, you **can't**.
Can	they	ski?	Yes, they **can**. / No, they **can't**.

4 Look at Nick's ability chart. Write the questions.

Activity	can (✓)	can't (✗)
swim	✓	
ski		✗
ride a bike	✓	
ice-skate		✗
jump high		✗
run fast	✓	

1 Can you ___swim___?
2 Can ______?
3 ______?
4 ______?
5 ______?
6 ______?

5 Write Nick's answers to the questions in exercise 4.

1 ___Yes, I can___. 4 ______.
2 ______. 5 ______.
3 ______. 6 ______.

Finished?
Page 96, Puzzle 6A

Over to you!

6 Ask and answer in class with *Can you …* ?

Student A: Can you dance?
Student B: Yes, I can. / No, I can't.

Tell the class about student B.
Nico can dance. He can't ski.

Building the topic

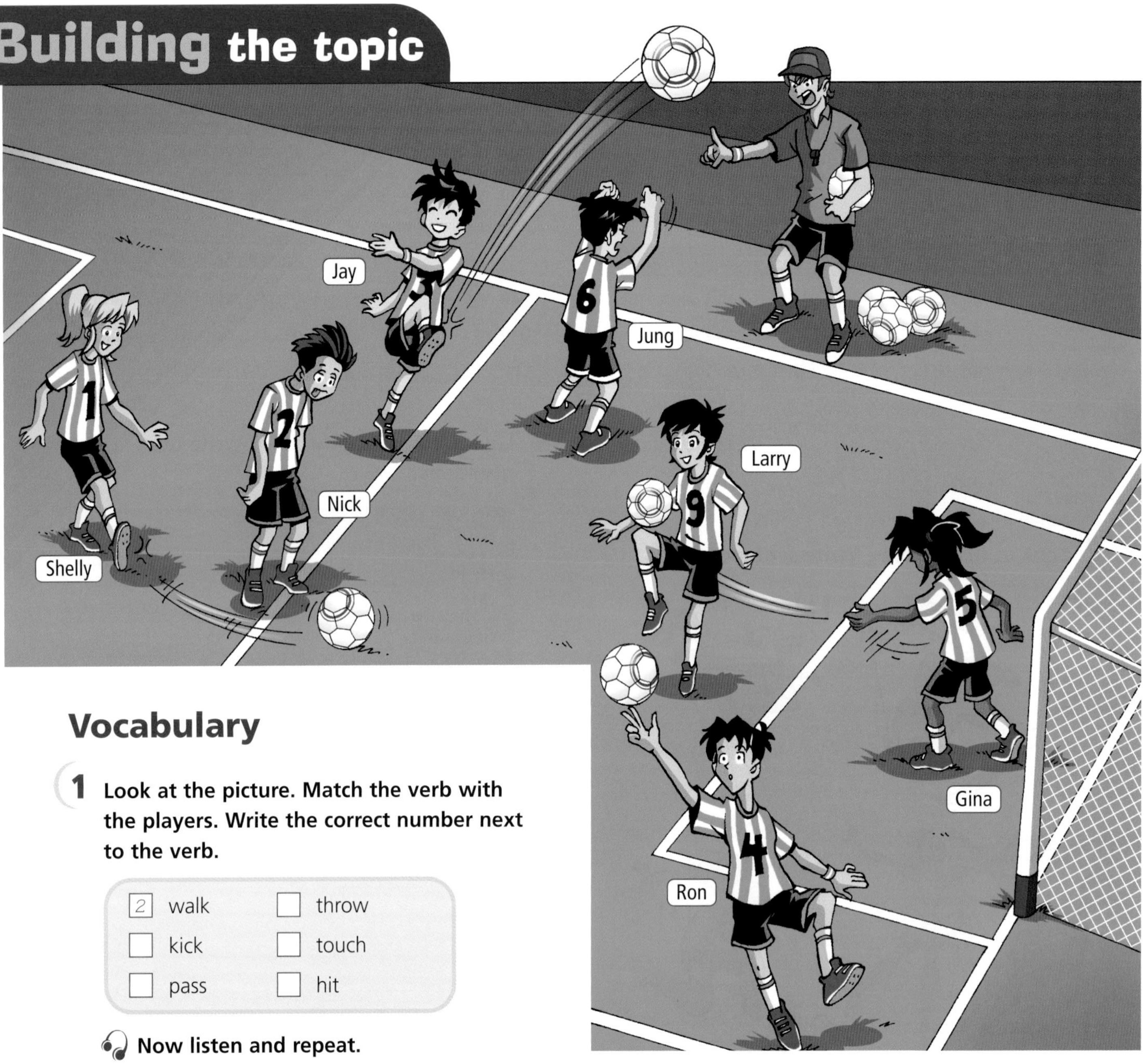

Vocabulary

1 Look at the picture. Match the verb with the players. Write the correct number next to the verb.

2	walk	☐	throw
☐	kick	☐	touch
☐	pass	☐	hit

Now listen and repeat.

2 Read and listen to the instructions. Then write the names.

Pass the ball to Nick!
1 Shelly
Don't hit the coach!
2
Don't touch the ball!
3
Kick the ball!
4
Run! Don't walk!
5
Throw the ball to Larry!
6

Grammar

Imperatives

Giving instructions

1 Look at the chart.

Affirmative	Negative
Run!	**Don't run**!
Pass the ball!	**Don't pass** the ball!

2 Look at the pictures. Write the instructions. Use the affirmative (✓) or negative (✗).

1 *Don't throw* the ball.

2 ________________ the ball.

3 ________________ the ball.

4 ________________ the ball.

5 ________________________!

3 Look at the signs. Write the instructions. Use the affirmative or negative.

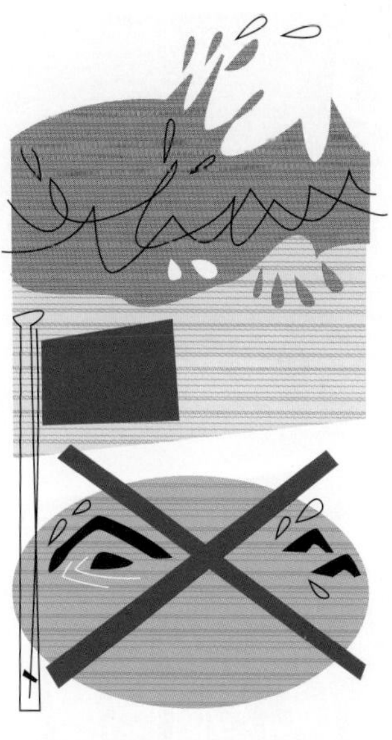

1 *Don't swim*.

2 ________________.

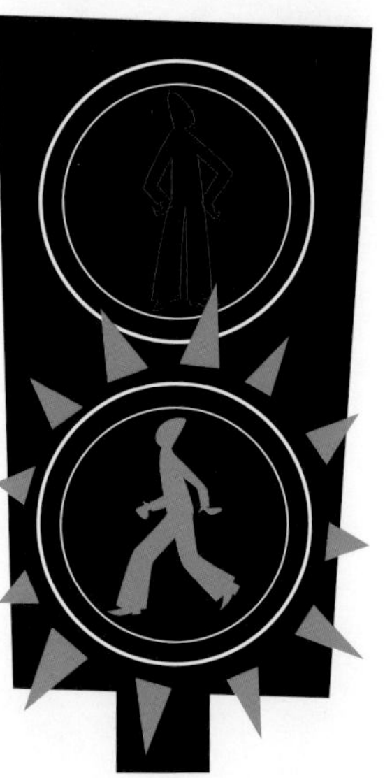

3 ________________.

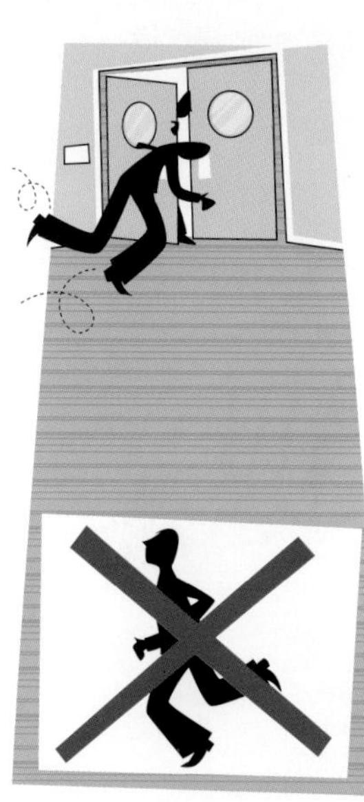

4 ________________.

Finished?
Page 96, Puzzle 6B

Over to you!

4 Find 3 instructions in this unit.

Look, …

Write 3 instructions for your classroom. Use the affirmative or the negative.

Don't throw paper on the floor.

Living English

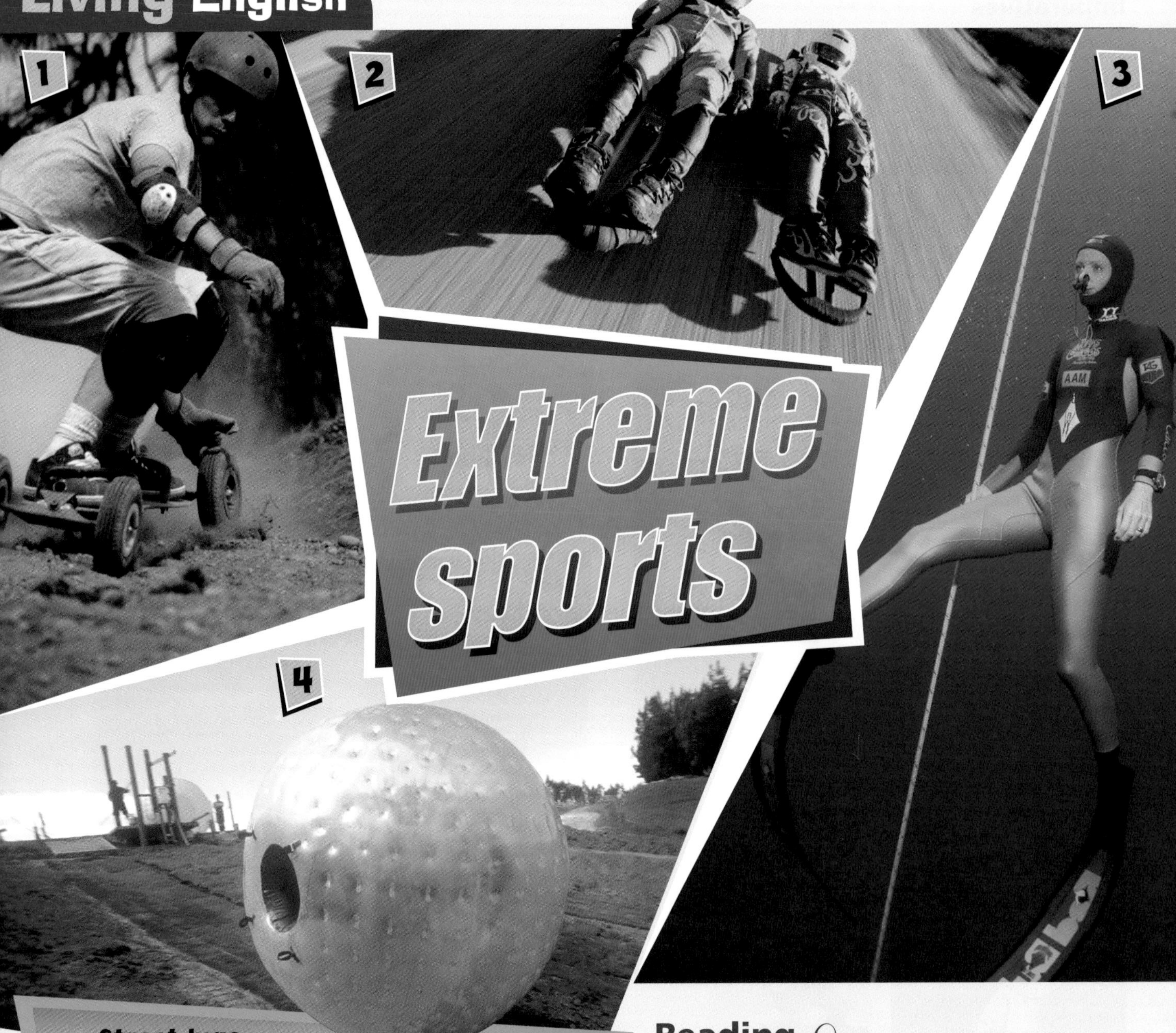

A Street luge

This sport is from the United States. The world champion is David Dean and he is American. He can go 100 kilometers per hour!

B Free diving

Tanya Streeter is the free diving world champion. She is British. She can dive 122 meters!

C Zorb ball

This sport is from New Zealand. Three people can go in a Zorb ball. It can go 60 kilometers per hour.
Rich Eley, from the United Kingdom, can go 323 meters in a Zorb ball!

D Mountainboarding

Tom Kirkman is the mountainboard world champion. He's from the United Kingdom. He can jump nine meters!

Reading

1 Look at the photos and read the texts. Match the photo with the text.

1 *D* 2 ___ 3 ___ 4 ___

2 Read again. Correct the information in blue.

1 Tom Kirkman is the Zorb ball world champion.
Tom Kirkman is the mountainboard world champion.
2 He can jump nineteen meters.
3 Zorb ball is from the United States.
4 Six people can go in a Zorb ball.
5 Street luge is from New Zealand.
6 Rich Eley is from the United States.
7 David Dean can go 200 kilometers per hour.
8 Tanya Streeter can dive 150 meters.

Writing

1 Look at the Writing skills box.

Writing skills

and and *but*

We use *and* to join similar ideas.

I can swim **and** I can ride a bike.

We use *but* to join contrasting ideas.

I can swim, **but** I can't ride a bike.

2 Now read the text. Circle the examples of *and* and *but*.

My name's Julia. I can swim, (but) I can't ice-skate.
My friends are Tom and Sarah. Tom can run fast and he can jump high! He's awesome. Sarah can dance, but she can't ice-skate. She's great.

3 Fill in the chart with information about Julia and her friends.

Name	can	can't
Julia	*swim*	*ice-skate*
Tom		✗
Sarah		
you		
Friend 1		
Friend 2		

4 Now fill in the chart with information about you and your friends.

5 Write about you and your friends. Use the text and the chart to help you.

Speaking

1 Listen and read.

Virtual, can you jump high?
Yes, I can!
Brainy, can you jump high?
No, I can't. But I can dance!

2 Look at the Pronunciation box. Listen to the examples.

Pronunciation

can

In the affirmative and questions, we pronounce *can* as /kən/.
In short answers, we pronounce *can* as /kæn/.

/kən/	/kæn/
Can you jump high?	Yes, I **can**.
I **can** dance.	

Listen again and repeat.

3 Listen. Check (✓) the correct column.

	/kən/	/kæn/
1 Can you ride a bike?	✓	
2 I can ski.		
3 Yes, I can.		
4 Can you ski?		

4 Practice the dialog with your partner.

5 Change the words in blue. Write a new dialog. Now practice the dialog in class.

Review 3

Vocabulary

Objects and furniture

1 Find ten objects in the word snake.

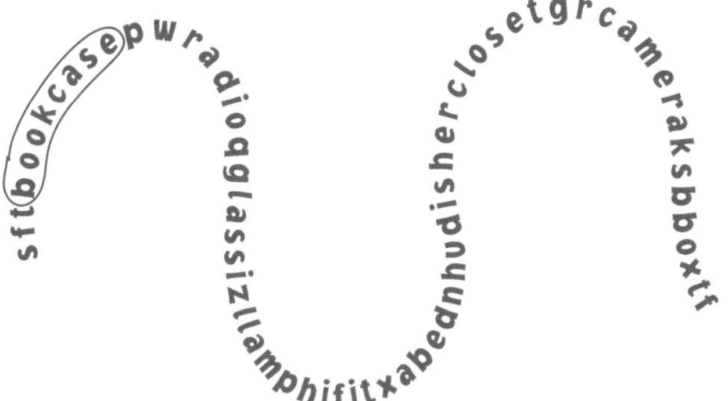

Abilities and sports rules

2 Unscramble the verbs.

1 ecadn ___dance___
2 mwis ______
3 ith ______
4 eird a reohs ______
5 kkci ______
6 isk ______
7 upjm gihh ______
8 hwotr ______
9 uhotc ______
10 lwka ______

Grammar

this / that / these / those

1 Fill in the blanks with *this, that, these* or *those*.

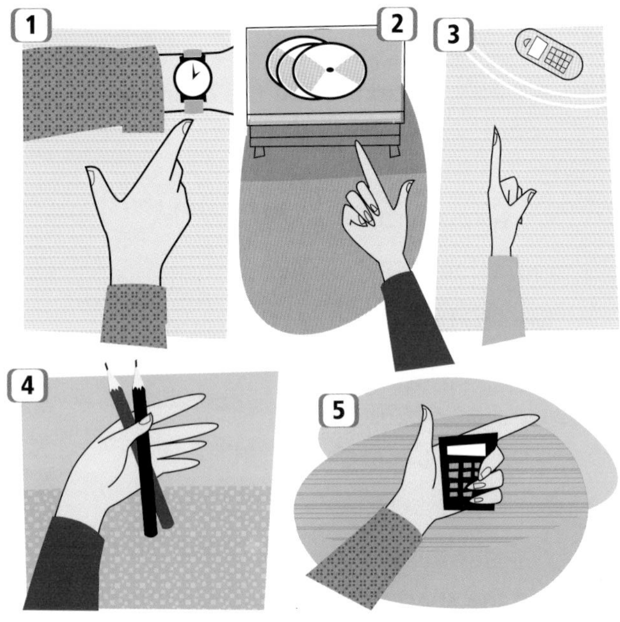

1 ___This___ is my watch.
2 ______ are my CDs.
3 ______ is my cell phone.
4 ______ are my pencils.
5 ______ is my calculator.

Plurals

2 Read the text. Fill in the blanks with the singular or plural of the words in parentheses.

Our classroom isn't very big, but it has a lot of things in it. There are three big (1) ___windows___ (window) and two (2) ______ (door). There are thirty-five (3) ______ (desk) for the students, and there is a (4) ______ (desk) for the teacher, too. There are three (5) ______ (clock) on the wall – I don't know why! There's a (6) ______ (bookcase) in the room, too. It has a lot of (7) ______ (book), some (8) ______ (glass) and some (9) ______ (dish) in it.

can / can't

3 Complete the dialogs.

1 **Ann:** *Can you speak* (you / speak) French, Tom?

Tom: No, I ________. But I ________ (speak) Spanish and Italian.

2 **Pedro:** ________ (Alicia and Magda / run) fast?

Geraldo: Yes, ________. But they ________ (not jump high).

3 **Toru:** ________ (your father / do) karate?

Sakura: No, ________. But he ________ (do) judo.

4 **Mai:** ________ (we / win) this game?

Hong: Yes, ________. We ________ (win) because we are great!

Imperatives

4 Look at the signs. Write imperatives. Use the words below.

play music   kick balls   ride bicycles
swim   walk with your dog
throw trash in the trash can

1 *Don't play music*. 2 ________.

3 ________. 4 ________.

5 ________. 6 ________.

Study skills

Spelling

In your notebook, make a list of difficult words. Practice spelling the words.

1 Look at these words from unit 5. Correct the spelling mistakes.

1 calculater *o*
2 televition
3 glas
4 watsh
5 tabel
6 telefone

2 Look at pages 42 and 44. Choose five difficult words. Add the words to your list and practice spelling them. Ask a friend to help you.

7 Day to day

Grammar: simple present (affirmative); simple present (*he* / *she* / *it*)
Vocabulary: daily activities

Exploring the topic

Vocabulary

1 Look at the pictures. Fill in the blanks with the words below.

go to school   get up   go to bed   watch TV
start classes   finish classes   have dinner
do my homework   have breakfast   have lunch

Now listen and repeat.

Take note!

at* / *in
at seven thirty / nine o'clock
in the morning / afternoon / evening

2 Fill in the blanks with *at* or *in*.

1 I get up _at_ seven o'clock.
2 I do my homework ______ the evening.
3 I have breakfast ______ the morning.
4 I have dinner ______ seven thirty.

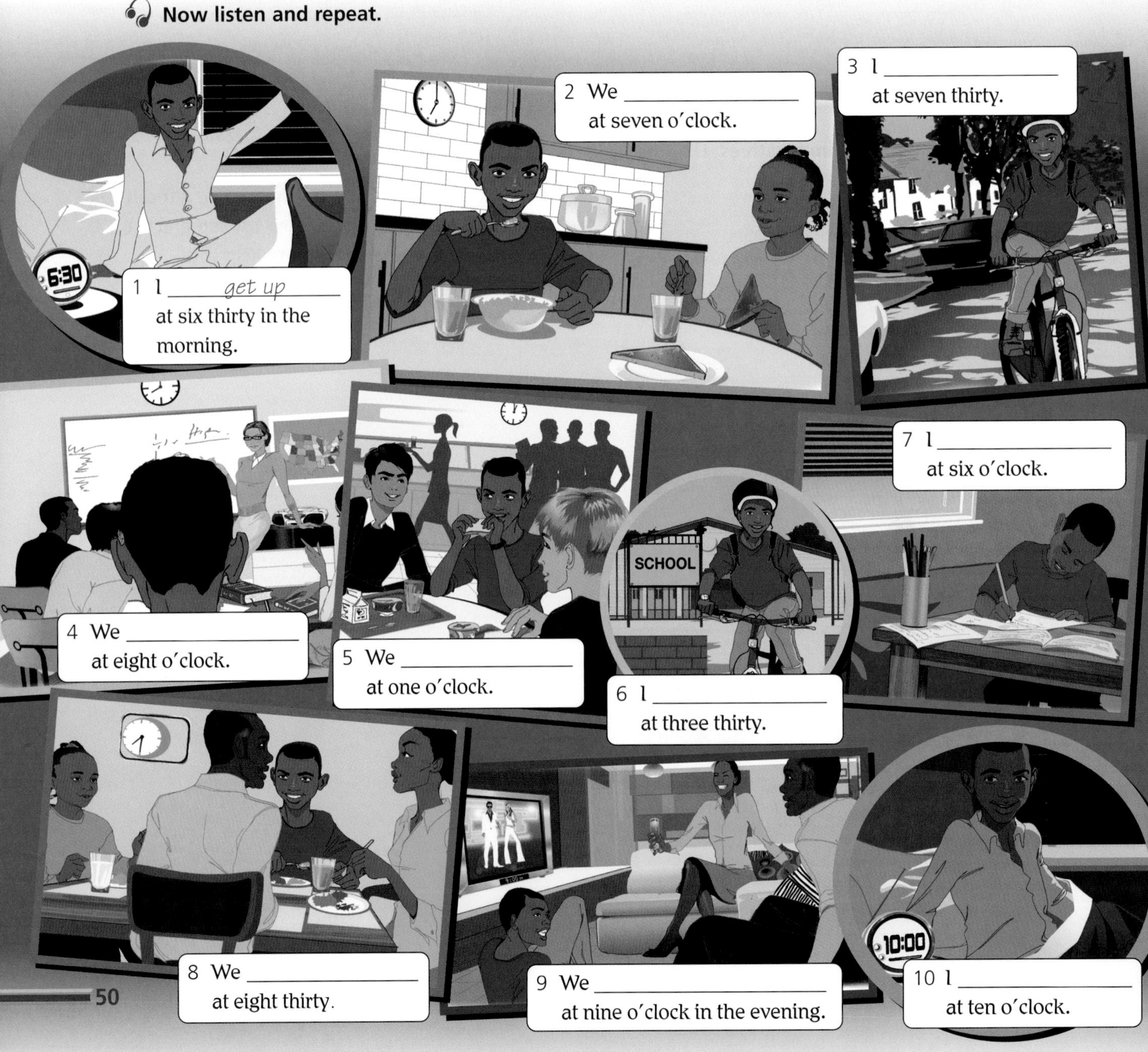

6:30
1 I _get up_ at six thirty in the morning.
2 We ________________ at seven o'clock.
3 I ________________ at seven thirty.
4 We ________________ at eight o'clock.
5 We ________________ at one o'clock.
SCHOOL
6 I ________________ at three thirty.
7 I ________________ at six o'clock.
8 We ________________ at eight thirty.
9 We ________________ at nine o'clock in the evening.
10:00
10 I ________________ at ten o'clock.

Grammar

Simple present (affirmative)

Talking about daily activities

1 Look at the chart.

Affirmative		
I	**go** to school	at eight o'clock.
You	**get** up	at seven thirty.
We	**have** lunch	at twelve thirty.
You	**watch** TV	in the evening.
They	**finish** classes	at three o'clock.

2 Look at the pictures. Write sentences.

1 We ___*get up*___ at seven o'clock.

2 We ______________ at seven thirty.

3 We ______________ at eight o'clock.

4 I ______________.

5 I ______________.

6 We ______________.

3 Fill in the blanks with the correct verbs.

In the morning, I (1) ___*get*___ up at six thirty. Then I (2) __________ breakfast. I (3) __________ to school and I (4) __________ classes at eight o'clock. I (5) __________ classes at three o'clock. After school, I (6) __________ my homework. I (7) __________ TV and I (8) __________ to bed.

Finished?
Page 98, Puzzle 7A

Over to you!

4 Write 3 true sentences and one false sentence about your daily routine. Can the class guess the false sentence?

Student A: I get up at seven thirty.
Student B: True! / False!

Building the topic

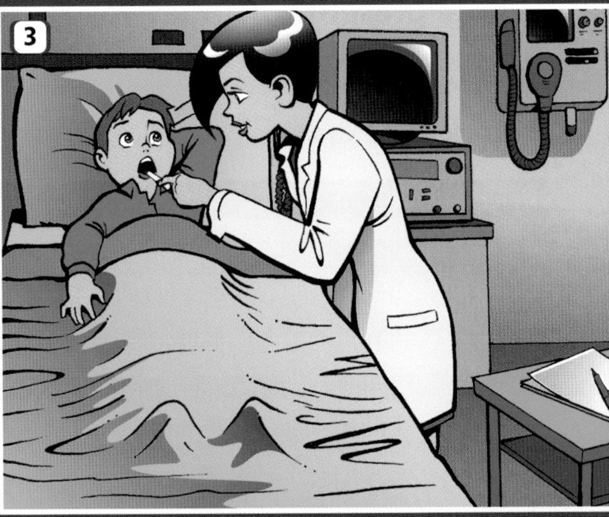

Vocabulary

1 Look at the pictures and read the text. Match the verbs below with the pictures.

paint surf read live love relax work meet

Picture 1: *live*

Picture 2: ____________

Picture 3: ____________ ____________

Picture 4: ____________ ____________ ____________

Picture 5: ____________

Now listen and repeat.

Amy Morillo lives in Hawaii. She gets up early every day and goes to the beach. She surfs and then she has breakfast.
Amy works in a children's hospital. She loves her job.
In the evening, Amy relaxes. She reads books, paints pictures and watches TV.
On the weekend, she meets her friends in a café.

2 Read and listen to the text. Then circle T (True) or F (False).

1 Amy lives in Barbados. T / (F)
2 She gets up early every day. T / F
3 She works in a school. T / F
4 She watches TV in the evening. T / F
5 She meets her friends on the weekend. T / F

Grammar

Simple present (*he* / *she* / *it*)

Talking about daily activities

1 Look at the chart.

Affirmative
add *-s*
He start**s** work at 9 o'clock.
She get**s** up at 7 o'clock.
It start**s** at 6 o'clock.
add *-es* after *-o*, *-x*, *-sh*, and *-ch*.
He watch**es** TV. / He do**es** his homework in the evening.
She relax**es**. / She go**es** to the beach on the weekend.
It finish**es** at 9 o'clock.
Irregular
He / She / It **has** breakfast in the morning.

2 Fill in the blanks with the correct form of the verb in parentheses.

1 He ___gets___ up at seven thirty. (get)
2 She __________ her homework in the evening. (do)
3 He __________ on the weekend. (relax)
4 He __________ his friends in the evening. (meet)
5 She __________ in a school. (work)
6 She __________ her job. (love)

3 Look at the pictures. Fill in the blanks with the correct form of the verb.

1 I ___paint___ on the weekend. (paint)

2 She __________ in the evening. (read)

3 They __________ dinner at seven o'clock. (have)

4 He __________ in Mexico. (live)

5 We __________ on the weekend. (surf)

6 He __________ breakfast at eight o'clock. (have)

4 Look at Lisa's timetable. Write sentences with the *he* / *she* / *it* form of the verb.

Monday
play tennis

Tuesday
swim

Wednesday
surf

Thursday
play soccer

Friday
meet my friends

1 On Monday, she ___plays tennis___.
2 On Tuesday, she __________.
3 __________.
4 __________.
5 __________.

Finished?
Page 98, Puzzle 7B

Over to you!

5 Write 3 sentences about your daily routine. Exchange your sentences in class.

Tell the class about another student.

Umberto gets up at seven o'clock.

Living English

Different countries, different lives

My name's Hyun and I'm fourteen. I live in Seoul. I get up at six thirty and I walk to school with my friends. I start classes at eight o'clock and finish at four o'clock. We have lunch at twelve o'clock. After school I do my homework and I have dinner with my family. I watch TV and I go to bed at eleven o'clock.

On Saturday I go to school. I start classes at eight o'clock and finish at twelve o'clock. Then I meet my friends and we play computer games.

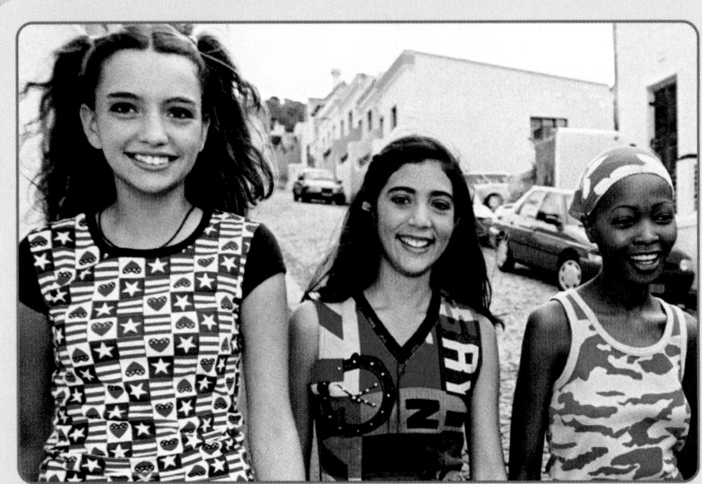

My name's Adriana. I'm thirteen and I'm from Rio de Janeiro. I get up at six o'clock in the morning. I take the bus to school. My classes start at seven and finish at two. We have lunch at twelve thirty. My friends and I play soccer after school. I do my homework in the evening, and I go to bed at ten thirty.

On Saturday, I meet my friends and we go to the beach.

Reading

1 **Read the texts. How old is Hyun? How old is Adriana?**

2 **Read again. Fill in the blanks in the chart.**

	Hyun	Adriana
gets up	(1) *6.30 a.m.*	6:00 a.m.
starts classes	8:00 a.m.	(2) ________
has lunch	(3) ________	(4) ________
finishes classes	(5) ________	2 p.m.
goes to bed	11:00 p.m.	(6) ________

3 **Read again. Write H (Hyun), A (Adriana) or B (both).**

1 "I get up at six o'clock." *A*
2 "I walk to school." ___
3 "I go to bed at eleven o'clock." ___
4 "I start classes at eight o'clock." ___
5 "I do my homework in the evening." ___
6 "I go to school on Saturday." ___
7 "I play soccer after school." ___
8 "I meet my friends on Saturday." ___

Listening

1 **Listen. Where is Cristina from? Where is she now?**

2 **Listen again. Check (✓) the correct column(s).**

	In Spain	In the United States
She gets up at seven thirty.		✓
She has lunch at two o'clock.		
She goes to the mall after school.		
She gets up late on the weekend.		
She goes to the beach on the weekend.		

Writing

1 **Look at the Writing skills box.**

Writing skills

then

We use *then* for sequences.

I get up at seven o'clock.
Then I have breakfast.

I get up at seven o'clock, and **then** I have breakfast.

2 **Read the e-mail. Circle the examples of *then*.**

Dear Emilia,

How are you?

This is my day. In the morning, I get up at seven and I have breakfast. (Then) I go to school. I start classes at eight o'clock. I have lunch at twelve thirty.

In the afternoon, I finish classes at three thirty. Then my friends and I play soccer or play computer games.

In the evening, I have dinner at six thirty. I do my homework, and then I go to bed.

What about you?

Write soon

Damon

3 **Fill in the chart with information about Damon's day.**

	Damon's day	Your day
In the morning	*get up at seven*	
	have breakfast	
In the afternoon		
In the evening		

4 **Now fill in the chart with information about your day.**

5 **Write an e-mail about your day. Use the text and the chart to help you.**

8 Lifestyles

Grammar: simple present (negative); *have / has*
Vocabulary: activities (work); physical appearance

Exploring the topic

① Ben ② Larry and Jake ③ Anita ④ Ruth ⑤ James

Vocabulary

1 **Match the photos with the verbs below. Write the correct number next to the words.**

[4] interview people	[ ] rescue people	[ ] sing
[ ] climb mountains	[ ] take photos	

Now listen and repeat.

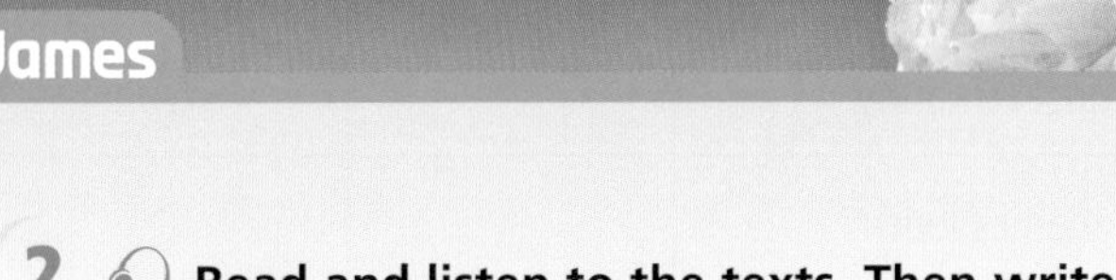

2 **Read and listen to the texts. Then write the names.**

Ⓐ He's a mountaineer. He doesn't ski. He climbs mountains. ___James___

Ⓑ He's a lifeguard. He rescues people. He doesn't have lunch at home. He has lunch on the beach. ___________

Ⓒ They're photographers. They don't interview people. They take photos. ___________ and ___________

Ⓓ She's a singer. She doesn't sing opera. She sings pop music. ___________

Ⓔ She's a TV host. She interviews people. She doesn't work in an office. She works in a TV studio. ___________

Grammar

Simple present (negative)

Talking about daily routines

1 Look at the chart.

Negative		
I	**don't**	interview people.
You	**don't**	rescue people.
He / She / It	**doesn't**	take photos.
We	**don't**	climb mountains.
You	**don't**	sing.
They	**don't**	work in an office.

2 Fill in the blanks with *don't* or *doesn't*.

1 We _don't_ live in Canada.
2 They ________ dance on the weekend.
3 He ________ get up at seven o'clock.
4 You ________ go to the beach on the weekend.
5 She ________ watch TV in the evening.

3 Correct the sentences about the people.

1 Leon sings in the evening. (paint)
Leon doesn't sing in the evening .
He paints in the evening .

2 Natalia interviews people. (take photos)
________________________________.
________________________________.

3 Joel plays basketball every day. (play soccer)
________________________________.
________________________________.

4 Dina dances in the afternoon. (ice-skate)
________________________________.
________________________________.

5 Richard works in an office. (work in a hospital)
________________________________.
________________________________.

6 Jason skis on Saturday. (surf)
________________________________.
________________________________.

Finished?
Page 98, Puzzle 8A

Over to you!

4 Write one negative and one affirmative sentence for each person. Use the verbs below.

People: I, my sister, my brother, my father, my friend

Verbs: interview people, work in an office, get up early, sing, watch TV, rescue people, surf, climb mountains, go to school

My mother doesn't rescue people.
She works in an office.

Building the topic

Vocabulary

1 **Find an example of each of the words below in the picture.**

Example: blue eyes: *number 2*

Eyes: blue brown green
Hair: short long straight wavy curly blond dark

Now listen and repeat.

Take note!

He's tall. He's short.

2 **Read and listen to the texts. Label the people with the correct names.**

Luis and Rob are tall. Luis has green eyes and short, blond hair. Rob has green eyes but he doesn't have blond hair. He has short, dark hair.

Christine and Nicky are short. They have blue eyes. Christine has long, straight hair. Nicky doesn't have straight hair. She has long, wavy hair.

Bruce and Steven are tall. Bruce has brown eyes and short, curly hair. Steven doesn't have brown eyes and he doesn't have curly hair. He has blue eyes and short, straight hair.

3 **Fill in the blanks with the words below.**

dark blond blue straight

1 Rob and Luis have short, *straight* hair.
2 Christine and Nicky have long, ________ hair.
3 Bruce and Steven have short, ________ hair.
4 Steven has ________ eyes.

Grammar

have / has

Talking about physical appearance

1 **Look at the chart.**

Affirmative	Negative
I **have** short hair.	I **don't have** short hair.
You **have** long hair.	You **don't have** short hair.
He / She / It **has** blond hair.	He / She / It **doesn't have** blond hair.
We **have** curly hair.	We **don't have** curly hair.
You **have** straight hair.	You **don't have** straight hair.
They **have** wavy hair.	They **don't have** wavy hair.

2 **Look at the other people from the party. Fill in the blanks with *have*, *has*, *don't have* or *doesn't have*.**

1 Carlos ___has___ blue eyes.
2 Carlos __________ straight hair.
3 Paula __________ brown eyes.
4 Maria and Paula __________ blond hair.
5 Jimmy __________ brown hair.
6 Paula and Jimmy __________ wavy hair.

3 **Fill in the blanks with *am*, *is*, *are*, *has* or *have*.**

1 I ___am___ short.
2 She ________ blond hair.
3 We ________ tall.
4 They ________ green eyes.
5 He ________ dark hair.
6 They ________ tall.

4 **Look at the picture. Correct the sentences.**

1 Miguel has short, dark hair.
Miguel doesn't have short, dark hair.
He has long, dark hair.

2 Renata has blue eyes.
__________________________.
__________________________.

3 Renata has short, straight hair.
__________________________.
__________________________.

4 Ben and Paul have blue eyes.
__________________________.
__________________________.

5 Jan and Candy have blond hair.
__________________________.
__________________________.

Finished?
Page 98, Puzzle 8B

Over to you!

5 **Describe your best friend. Tell the class.**

My best friend is Helena. She is tall. She has green eyes. She has long, blond hair.

Living English

Extraordinary teens

Matt is fifteen and lives in Manhattan. He plays the guitar and writes rock songs for a band called "Genius". Matt doesn't go to a regular school. He goes to a music school.
"Genius" travels to concerts on a bus. The kids do their homework on the bus.

Andrea is fourteen and lives in Mexico. She's a model for a TV fashion show. She gets up very early in the morning and goes to the TV studio. She goes to school in the afternoon. Andrea doesn't go out on the weekend. She rides her bike and meets her friends.

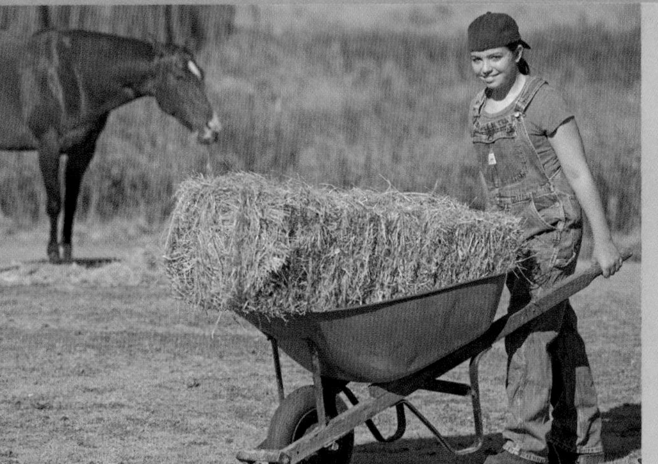

Jess is sixteen and lives in a very small village on a mountain in Canada. She works on a farm early in the morning. Jess doesn't go to school. The teacher comes to her house! On the weekend, Jess climbs the mountain, rides her bike and plays games.

Reading

1 Look at the Reading skills box.

Reading skills
Scanning
You can read the text quickly to find information.

Now read the text quickly and fill in the blanks below.

1 Matt lives in *Manhattan*.
2 Andrea lives in ________________.
3 Jess lives in ________________.

2 Read the texts and write the correct name(s) next to the sentences.

1 She works in a TV studio. *Andrea*
2 They don't go to a regular school.
________________ and ________________
3 He writes songs. ________________
4 He does his homework on a bus.
____
5 She doesn't go out on the weekend.
____
6 She lives on a mountain. ________________

3 Circle T (True) or F (False). Correct the false sentences.

1 Matt writes hip hop songs. T / (F)
Matt doesn't write hip hop songs. He writes rock songs.
2 "Genius" travels on a bus. T / F
3 Andrea gets up very early in the morning. T / F
4 She goes to school in the morning. T / F
5 Jess works in a store. T / F
6 She climbs the mountain on the weekend. T / F

Listening

1 Listen and write the correct name under the pictures.

Captain Cool   Mister Fantastic   Super Simon

2 Now listen and write ✓ or ✗ in the chart below.

	gets up early	works in an office	rescues people
Captain Cool	✓		
Super Simon			
Mister Fantastic			

Speaking

1 Listen and read.

Tell me about your sister, Electrica.

Well, she's great. She climbs mountains and takes photos.

Wow!

And she goes to the beach and she watches TV.

2 Look at the Pronunciation box. Listen to the examples.

Pronunciation

Simple present

The pronunciation of simple present *-s* is different for different verbs.

/s/	/z/	/ɪz/
take**s**	climb**s**	watch**es**

Listen again and repeat.

3 Listen. Put the verbs in the correct column.

rescues   relaxes   gets   interviews   paints

/s/	/z/	/ɪz/
	rescues	

4 Practice the dialog with your partner.

5 Change the words in blue. Write a new dialog. Now practice the dialog in class.

Review 4

Vocabulary

Daily activities

1 Fill in the blanks in the sentences. Use the words from the box.

go start live have watch finish
paint surf do get up

1 We ___start___ classes at eight in the morning and we __________ classes at three in the afternoon.
2 After school, I __________ my homework and then I __________ TV.
3 I __________ in Hawaii. I __________ to the beach and I __________ in the ocean every day.
4 On the weekend, we __________ pictures.
5 I __________ at half past six and then I __________ breakfast.

Activities (work)

2 Match 1–5 with A–E.

1 He's a singer. _D_
2 He's a lifeguard. ___
3 He's a photographer. ___
4 He's a TV host. ___
5 He's a mountaineer. ___

A He rescues people.
B He climbs mountains.
C He takes photos.
D He sings.
E He interviews people.

Physical appearance

3 Look at the pictures. Write A or B next to the words.

1 green eyes _A_
2 blond hair ___
3 wavy hair ___
4 straight hair ___
5 blue eyes ___
6 dark hair ___
7 short hair ___
8 tall ___
9 long hair ___
10 short ___

Grammar

Simple present (affirmative)

1 Fill in the blanks with the correct form of the verbs below.

have go paint sing work take

1 My friend, Dana, and I ___sing___ in a pop group.
2 Chen and Jung are photographers. They __________ photos.
3 I __________ lunch at one o'clock.
4 She __________ pictures on the weekend.
5 You __________ in a hospital.
6 He __________ to school at eight o'clock.

Simple present (negative)

2 **Look at the chart. Write sentences with the simple present affirmative and negative.**

	get up early	have breakfast	watch TV	play soccer	go to bed at ten o'clock
Andrea	✓	✗	✓	✓	✗
Mark	✗	✓	✗	✓	✗

1 *Andrea gets up early* .
Mark doesn't get up early .
2 ______ .
______ .
3 ______ .
______ .
4 ______ .
______ .
5 ______ .
______ .

have / has

3 **Write full sentences with *has, have, don't have* or *doesn't have*.**

1 Larry / have / a computer.
Larry has a computer .
2 Maria and Lisa / not have / cell phones.
______ .
3 Tamsin / not have / an iPod.
______ .
4 We / not have / skateboards.
______ .
5 Luis and Gabrielle / have / cameras.
______ .
6 Antonio / have / an eraser.
______ .

Study skills

Grammar

In your notebook, make a grammar section. Write examples, translations and explanations in your language. Write examples of your mistakes.

1 **Look at the notes.**

+ s He gets up at 3:30.
+ es She watches TV.
bad: ~~She start school at 9 o'clock.~~
good: She starts school at 9 o'clock.

Is the grammar point:
1 simple present *he / she / it*?
2 simple present negative?
3 simple present questions?

2 **Make notes on the simple present in your notebook.**

9 Entertainment

Grammar: simple present (*yes / no* questions); *like*
Vocabulary: places; movies and adjectives

Exploring the topic

Vocabulary

1 Label the photos with the words below.

concert dance club
sports club soccer game
theme park party
beach country

Now listen and repeat.

1 *soccer game*
2 ______
3 ______
4 ______
5 ______
6 ______
7 ______
8 ______

2 Read and listen to the questions. Then check ✓ (Yes, I do) or ✗ (No, I don't).

Do you... ?	Yes, I do. (✓)	No, I don't. (✗)
1 Do you go to concerts?	☐	☐
2 Do you go to dance clubs?	☐	☐
3 Do you go to a sports club?	☐	☐
4 Do you go to parties?	☐	☐
5 Do you go to theme parks?	☐	☐
6 Do you go to soccer games?	☐	☐
7 Do you go to the beach?	☐	☐
8 Do you go to the country?	☐	☐

3 Write sentences about your answers to the questions in exercise 2.

1 *I go to concerts*______. or
*I don't go to concerts*______.
2 ______.
3 ______.
4 ______.
5 ______.
6 ______.
7 ______.
8 ______.

Grammar

Simple present (*yes / no* questions)

Asking about regular activites

1 Look at the chart.

Question			Short answers
Do	I	go to dance clubs?	Yes, I **do**. / No, I **don't**.
Do	you	go to the beach?	Yes, you **do**. / No, you **don't**.
Does	he / she / it	go to soccer games?	Yes, he / she/ it **does**. / No, he / she / it **doesn't**.
Do	we	go to concerts?	Yes, we **do**. / No, we **don't**.
Do	you	go to soccer games?	Yes, you **do**. / No, you **don't**.
Do	they	go to a sports club?	Yes, they **do**. / No, they **don't**.

2 Put the words in order to make questions for pop singer Jessy.

1 you / to parties / Do / go

Do you go to parties ________?

2 go / you / to the beach / Do

________?

3 to the gym / you / go / Do

________?

4 go / Do / to concerts / you

________?

5 to dance clubs / Do / go / you

________?

3 Complete the interview with the questions from exercise 2.

You: Hi Jessy.
Jessy: Hi!
You: (1) *Do you go to concerts* ________?
Jessy: Yes, I do. I go to pop concerts.
You: (2) ________?
Jessy: No, I don't. I'm tired on the weekend. I don't go to parties.
You: (3) ________?
Jessy: Yes, I do. I go to the gym every day.
You: (4) ________?
Jessy: Yes, I do. I go to dance clubs on Saturday.
You: (5) ________?
Jessy: Yes, I do. I love the beach.

4 Write questions and answers for Jessy's friends.

1 Susy / sing?
Does Susy sing ________? Yes, *she does*.
2 Bill / go to concerts?
________? No, ________.
3 Susy and Karen / paint?
________? Yes, ________.
4 Bill and Karen / sing?
________? No, ________.
5 Bill / surf?
________? Yes, ________.
6 Susy and Bill / take photos?
________? Yes, ________.

Finished?
Page 99, Puzzle 9A

Over to you!

5 Ask and answer in class.

Student A: Do you go to concerts?
Student B: Yes, I do. or No, I don't.

Now tell the class about Student B.
Lara goes to concerts. She doesn't go to dance clubs.

Building the topic

Vocabulary

1 **Label the movie posters in the picture with the words below.**

science fiction movie   love story
horror movie   comedy   action movie

Now listen and repeat.

2 **Look at the dialogs. Fill in the blanks with the words below.**

funny   boring   scary   romantic   exciting

Now listen and repeat.

Grammar

like

Talking about likes and dislikes

1 **Look at the chart.**

Affirmative	Negative
He / She / It **likes** rap music.	He / She / It **doesn't like** rap music.
Question	**Answer**
Do they **like** concerts?	Yes, they **do**. / No, they **don't**.

2 **Look at the pictures. Fill in the blanks with *likes* or *doesn't like*.**

1 Glen ___likes___ rap music.
2 Brian ____________ rap music.

3 Ricardo ____________ computer games.
4 Luisa ____________ computer games.

5 Yuki ____________ love stories.
6 Mario ____________ love stories.

3 **Complete the questions and answers about the people in exercise 2.**

1 ___Does___ Glen ___like___ rap music?
Yes, ___he does___.
2 ________ Brian ________ rap music?
No, ______________.
3 ________ Ricardo ________ computer games? No, ______________.
4 ________ Luisa ________ computer games?
Yes, ______________.
5 ________ Yuki ________ love stories?
________, ______________.
6 ________ Mario ________ love stories?
________, ______________.

4 **Fill in the blanks with the words below.**

like likes do does don't doesn't

1 They ___like___ horror movies.
2 We ________ like love stories.
3 ________ she like science fiction movies?
4 He ________ rock music.
5 Does he like hip hop music? No, he ________.
6 ________ you like pop music?

Finished?
Page 99, Puzzle 9B

Over to you!

5 **Ask and answer in class. Use these words.**

action movies rap concerts soccer games love stories comedies

Student A: Do you like action movies?
Student B: Yes, I do. They're exciting.
Student A: Do you like rap?
Student B: No, I don't. It's boring.

Now tell the class about Student B.

Greg likes action movies, but he doesn't like rap.

Living English

Entertainment today

Theme Park
Go to 'Wild' theme park. It is open from 9 a.m. to 8 p.m.

Concert
See pop singer Jessy and hear her new album. Gigs, 9 p.m.

Dance Club
Dance and listen to hip hop from DJ Frankie Z. Angel Club, 8 p.m.

Sports
Learn to surf at Beachside Sports Club, 3 p.m.

Parties
Wear famous pop singers' clothes and sing at our music party. Megateen Club, 7 p.m.

Movies
Watch the new horror movie 'Vampire', Movie City, 5 p.m. and 7 p.m.

Games
Play new board games with your friends. Southtown Youth Club, 6 p.m.

Reading

1 Read the text. Answer the questions.

Where can you …

1 watch a movie? *Movie City*
2 dance? __________
3 surf? __________
4 play board games? __________
5 sing? __________
6 see a concert? __________

2 Read again. Complete the diary with the correct time or place.

3 March

9 a.m. (1) *'Wild' theme park*
(2) __________ *Beachside Sports Club*
6 p.m. (3) __________
(4) __________ *Megateen Club*
9 p.m. (5) __________

Writing

1 Look at the Writing skills box.

Writing skills

because

We use *because* to give reasons.

I like comedies because they're funny.

2 Read the text. Circle the examples of *because*.

I like pop music, but I don't like hip hop music. My favorite band is McFly because they're excellent. I like action movies because they're exciting.
My sister likes rock music, but she doesn't like pop music. Her favorite singer is Avril Lavigne. She likes love stories because they're romantic.

3 Fill in the chart with information about Katie and her sister.

	music	movies
Katie	*likes pop music*	*action movies – exciting*
	doesn't like hip hop music	
	favorite band McFly – excellent	
her sister		
me		
my sister / brother / friend		

4 Now fill in the chart with information about you and your sister / brother / friend.

5 Write about you and your sister / brother / friend. Use the text and the chart to help you.

Speaking

1 Listen and read.

2 Look at the Pronunciation box. Listen to the examples.

Pronunciation

Questions

Intonation goes up (↗) at the end of *yes / no* questions and down (↘) at the end of *wh-* questions.

Do you like rock music? ↗

What music do you like? ↘

Listen again and repeat.

3 Write ↗ for the *yes / no* questions, and ↘ for the *wh-* questions.

1 What movies do you like? ↘
2 Do you like horror movies?
3 What's your name?
4 Are you British?

Listen and repeat.

4 Practice the dialog with your partner.

5 Change the words in blue. Write a new dialog. Now practice the dialog in class.

10 Free time fun

Grammar: simple present (*wh*- questions); expressions of frequency
Vocabulary: parties; leisure activities

Exploring the topic

Vocabulary

1 Label the pictures with the words below.

decorate the room | make a cake | eat cake
play CDs | give presents | make cards
give a concert | wear nice clothes

Now listen and repeat.

Amata's party

Shogo's party

2 Write S for Shogo's party or A for Amata's party.

Now listen and check.

It's party time! Shogo and Amata talk about their special parties.

1 When do you have the party?
On the last day of school. *S*
On the first day of school. *A*

2 Where do you have the party?
In the school gym. ___
In our classroom. ___

3 What do you do before the party?
We make cards and we make a cake. ___
We decorate the room. ___

4 What do you do at the party?
We give presents. Then we play CDs and eat cake! ___
We give a concert and we wear nice clothes. ___

5 Why do you enjoy it?
Because it's the last day of school. ___
Because it's fun! ___

Grammar

Simple present (*wh-* questions)

Asking about regular activities

1 Look at the chart.

Questions			
What	**do**	**I**	**do?**
When	**do**	**you**	**start** classes?
Why	**does**	**he / she / it**	**have** the party?
How	**do**	**we**	**go** to school?
What	**do**	**you**	**do** at the party?
Where	**do**	**they**	**have** the party?

2 Match the answers with the questions.

Questions

1 What do you do on the weekend? _C_
2 When do you get up on school days? ___
3 Where do you meet your friends? ___
4 What do you do after school? ___
5 How do you go to school? ___
6 Why do you like school? ___

Answers

A We go to soccer practice and do our homework after school.
B Because we learn a lot and see our friends.
C We get up late, play games and watch movies on the weekend.
D We get up at seven in the morning.
E We meet our friends at a café.
F We take the bus to school.

3 Circle the correct question word.

1 (What) / Where do you celebrate in November?
We celebrate Thanksgiving.
2 How / When do they finish school?
They finish school in June.
3 Why / When do you have a party on January 14th?
Because it's my birthday!
4 How / What do you spell your name?
J-O-N-N-Y.
5 What / When does your teacher wear to school?
She wears nice clothes.
6 How / Where do you ride your bike?
I ride my bike in the park.

4 Write the questions for Susanna.

Susanna, 14, Mexico

You: (1) _When do you get up_ ?
Susanna: I get up at seven thirty.
You: (2) ________ to school?
Susanna: I ride my bike to school.
You: (3) ________ ?
Susanna: I start classes at eight thirty.
You: (4) ________ ?
Susanna: I have lunch at school.
You: (5) ________ after school?
Susanna: I meet my friends and we play basketball.
You: (6) ________ on the weekend?
Susanna: I wear jeans on the weekend.

Finished?
Page 101, Puzzle 10A

Over to you!

5 Write five questions with *What*, *When*, *Why*, *How*, and *Where*.
Ask and answer in class.

Student A: What do you do on the weekend?
Student B: I meet my friends and we play soccer.
Student A: Where do you have lunch?
Student B: I have lunch at school.

Building the topic

What do you do after school?

How often do you ...	0	1	2	3	4	5	7
go shopping?	✔						
go to the library?			✔				
go swimming?				✔			
read books?							✔
play a team sport?			✔				
go out with friends?		✔					
watch TV?					✔		
surf the Net?						✔	
play computer games?			✔				
talk on the phone?		✔					

0 = never 1 = once a week 2 = twice a week 3 = three times a week
4 = four times a week 5 = five times a week 7 = every day

Vocabulary

1 Match the photos with the words below. Write the correct number next to the words.

[9] go out with friends	[ ] go shopping
[ ] play a team sport	[ ] go swimming
[ ] talk on the phone	[ ] go to the library
[ ] surf the Net	[ ] watch TV
[ ] play computer games	[ ] read books

Now listen and repeat.

2 Read and listen to the questions above. Now look at the answers in the chart and fill in the blanks with the correct verbs.

1 I never ___go shopping___.
2 I ________________ three times a week.
3 I ________________ four times a week.
4 I ________________ five times a week.
5 I ________________ every day.

Grammar

Expressions of frequency

Talking about how often we do activities

1 **Look at the chart.**

Questions and answers
How often do you go swimming? I **never** go swimming. / I go swimming **twice a week**.
How often does he / she / it play a team sport? He plays a team sport **once a month**. She plays a team sport **three times a year**.

2 **Replace the words in *italics* with the expressions below.**

three times a year · once a month · twice a day · five times a week · twice a week · every day

1 They go swimming *every Monday and Friday*.
They go swimming twice a week.

2 He goes shopping *in January, June and October*.
____
______________________________.

3 We watch TV *every Tuesday, Thursday, Friday, Saturday and Sunday*.
____
______________________________.

4 I go to the library *once in January, once in February, once in March, etc*.
____
______________________________.

5 She surfs the Net *twice on Monday, twice on Tuesday, etc*.
____
______________________________.

6 You go out with friends *on Monday, Tuesday, Wednesday, Thursday, Friday, Saturday and Sunday*.
____
______________________________.

3 **Look at Victor's schedule. Complete the questions and answers.**

Monday	4p.m. tennis lesson
Tuesday	7p.m. guitar lesson
Wednesday	5p.m. go to the library
Thursday	7p.m. guitar lesson
Friday	4p.m. tennis lesson
Saturday	11a.m. guitar lesson
Sunday	2p.m. go swimming

1 How often do you have tennis lessons?
2 Twice a week.
3 ______________ have guitar lessons?
4 ______________.
5 ______________ go to the library?
6 ______________.
7 ______________ go swimming?
8 ______________.
9 ______________ relax?
10 I ______________ relax!

Finished?
Page 101, Puzzle 10B

Over to you!

4 **Ask and answer in class about your free time activities.**

Student A: I play soccer.
Student B: How often do you play soccer?
Student A: Three times a week.

Living English

Free time around the world

1 Tiffany, 15, the United States, cheerleader

Q Why do you like cheerleading?
A I like it because it's good exercise and because I make a lot of friends.
Q How often do you practice?
A We practice three times a week. And we sing and dance at games two or three times a week.

2 Taro, 14, Japan, karaoke singer

Q What is karaoke?
A The DJ plays a famous song on CD, but there isn't any singing. So you are the singer!
Q Why do you enjoy karaoke?
A Because I can sing for people. And it's fun.
Q Where do you sing?
A I sing at a local youth club.
Q How often do you do karaoke?
A I do karaoke two or three times a week.
Q Do you have competitions in your club?
A No, we don't. We just do it for fun.

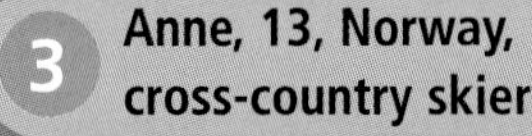

3 Anne, 13, Norway, cross-country skier

Q Why do you ski?
A Well, there's a lot of snow in Norway, so it's a good activity.
Q Where do you ski?
A I ski in the country around our town.
Q Why do you like skiing?
A Skiing is great. You go fast and it's good exercise.
Q How often do you ski?
A I ski every day in winter. I ski to school!

Reading

1 Look at the Reading skills box.

Reading skills
Using dictionaries
You can use a dictionary to find words that you don't know.

Put the words in alphabetical order.

cheerleader *1* snow ☐
nature ☐ competition ☐ country ☐

Now find the words in your dictionary. Write the meaning in your language.

2 Read the text. Is the text about:
1 cheerleading? 2 hobbies? 3 sports?

3 Read again. Then answer the questions.
1 What is Tiffany's hobby?
Cheerleading.
2 How often does Tiffany practice?
3 What is Taro's hobby?
4 Where does he do his hobby?
5 How often does he do his hobby?
6 What is Anne's hobby?
7 How often does she do her hobby?
8 How does Anne go to school in winter?

Listening

1 Listen to the dialog. Complete the chart with Mark's answers.

How often do you …	Never	Twice a week	Once a month
go out with friends?			
play a team sport?			
go to the movies?			
go to concerts?			

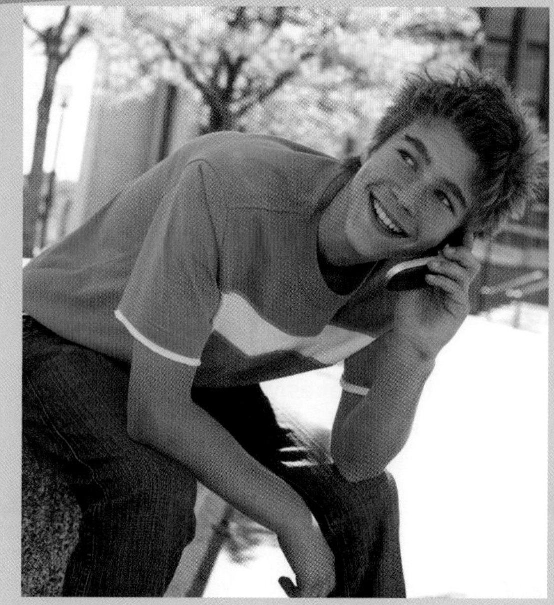

2 Listen again. Circle T (True) or F (False).

1 Mark goes to the mall with his friends twice a week. (T) / F
2 He plays basketball twice a week. T / F
3 He likes science fiction movies. T / F
4 He doesn't like rock music. T / F

Speaking

1 Listen and read.

2 Look at the Pronunciation box. Listen to the example.

Pronunciation

Silent letters

Some words have 'silent' letters.

of~~t~~en

Listen again and repeat.

3 Listen. Cross out the silent letters.

1 clim~~b~~ 2 walk 3 listen

4 Practice the dialog with your partner.

5 Change the words in blue. Write a new dialog. Now practice the dialog in class.

Review 5

Vocabulary

Places

1 Complete the words.

1 c o n c e r t
2 s _ _ _ _ _   _ _ _ e
3 s _ _ _ _ _   c _ _ _
4 _ _ _ _ e   c _ _ _
5 _ _ _ _ h
6 _ _ _ _ y
7 _ _ u _ _ _ _
8 _ _ _ _ e   _ _ _ _

Movies and adjectives

2 Label the pictures. Use one movie type and one adjective for each picture.

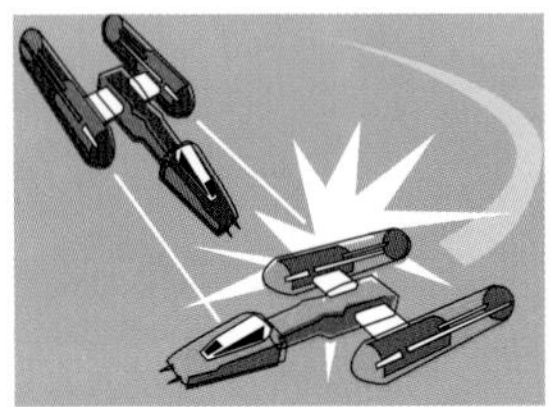

1 science fiction
exciting

2 ________
____

3 ________
____

4 ________
____

Parties and leisure activities

3 Match 1–10 with A–J.

1 give	A on the phone
2 watch	B the Net
3 read	C presents
4 surf	D nice clothes
5 decorate	E shopping
6 talk	F the room
7 wear	G books
8 play	H TV
9 eat	I computer games
10 go	J cake

Grammar

Simple present (*yes* / *no* questions)

1 Fill in the blanks with *do* or *does*. Then match the questions with the answers.

1 Do you go to dance clubs?
2 ________ your friends go to the beach?
3 ________ your brother go to soccer games?
4 ________ you go to a sports club?
5 ________ your sister go swimming?
6 ________ your parents surf the Net?

A No, she doesn't. ___
B Yes, they do. They like the beach. ___
C Yes, I do. 1
D No, they don't. ___
E No, I don't. ___
F Yes, he does. ___

like

2 Correct the mistakes with *like*. There is one mistake in each sentence.

Hi Pam.
(1) Thanks for writing about your favorite movies. I ~~likes~~ love stories, too. like
(2) I don't like horror movies, but my brother like them a lot. ________
(3) He don't like action movies , but I do. ________
(4) My parents doesn't like action movies or horror movies. ________
(5) We all likes comedies, and we watch them together. ________
(6) Does you like *The Lord of the Rings*? ________
It's my favorite movie. Viggo Mortenson is cool!
Take care,
Grace

Simple present (*wh-* questions)

3 Write the questions for Alex. Use the words in parentheses.

A: (1) *What do you and your sister do* in the summer, Alex? (what / you and your sister/ do)

B: Well, we go to different places.

A: Really? (2) ______________________? (where / you / go)

B: I go to my grandparents' house.

A: (3) ______________________? (where / they / live)

B: They live in Alaska.

A: Wow! (4) ______________________ there? (how / you / go)

B: I fly.

A: What about your sister? (5) ______________ ______________? (where / she / go)

B: She goes to a sports camp.

A: That's cool. (6) ______________________? (what / she / play)

B: She plays tennis. She's really good.

Expressions of frequency

4 Look at Kim's schedule. Write sentences. Use the words in parentheses.

Monday	Tuesday	Wednesday	Thursday	Friday	Saturday	Sunday
soccer practice	guitar lessons	soccer practice		soccer practice	meet friends at mall	visit grand-parents
	gym		gym	library	TV	TV

1 Kim *goes to the library once a week*.
(go to the library)

2 Kim ______________________.
(go to the museum)

3 ______________________.
(play soccer)

4 ______________________.
(meet her friends at the mall)

5 ______________________.
(visit her grandparents)

6 ______________________.
(go to the gym)

Study skills

Using your coursebook

***Engage* has different types of material to help you study.**

1 Look at this list. Where can you find these things?

1 "I want to study new vocabulary for units 9 and 10."
2 "I want to study grammar explanations for units 9 and 10."
3 "I want extra reading for units 7–9."
4 "I want project work for units 7–9."

a Grammar summary (page 107)
b Engage Magazine (page 100)
c Engage Magazine (page 99)
d Wordlist (page 111)

11 Reality show

Grammar: present progressive (affirmative); present progressive (negative)
Vocabulary: actions; rooms in a house

Exploring the topic

Vocabulary

1 Look at the pictures. Fill in the blanks with the words below.

falling pushing pulling closing opening
laughing shouting dropping

Now listen and repeat.

2 Match the verb with the *-ing* form.

1	close	a	pushing
2	open	b	laughing
3	push	c	dropping
4	laugh	d	opening
5	shout	e	falling
6	pull	f	closing
7	drop	g	pulling
8	fall	h	shouting

1 **Silvia**
She's ______________ the window.
2 **Pedro**
He's ______________ the door.
3 **Paul**
He's ______________ the door.
4 **David and Jasmin**
They're ______________ a towel.
5 **Melanie**
She's ______________.
6 **Lara**
She's ______________ a glass.
7 **Julio**
He's ______________.
8 **Marty and Ferdinand**
They're ______________.

Grammar

Present progressive (affirmative)

Talking about now

1 **Look at the chart.**

Affirmative	
I'**m**	dropp**ing** a glass.
You'**re**	fall**ing**.
He'**s** / She'**s** / It'**s**	push**ing** a door.
We'**re**	clos**ing** a window.
You'**re**	laugh**ing**.
They'**re**	shout**ing**.

Take note!

Spelling rules for *-ing* forms

Regular: add *-ing*.
fall ➔ **falling**

Consonant + *-e*: *-e̸* + *-ing*.
close ➔ **closing**

One vowel + one consonant: double the consonant + *-ing*.
drop ➔ **dropping**

2 **Write the *-ing* form of the verbs.**

1 dance *dancing*
2 surf ______
3 climb ______
4 wear ______
5 decorate ______
6 chat ______
7 watch ______
8 make ______
9 sing ______

3 **Fill in the blanks with the correct form of *be*. Use short forms.**

1 We *'re* shouting.
2 They ______ laughing.
3 I ______ reading a book.
4 She ______ making a cake.
5 He ______ climbing a mountain.
6 You ______ surfing the Net.

4 **Write the sentences. Use short forms.**

1 *He's watching TV* ______.
2 ______.
3 ______.
4 ______.
5 ______.
6 ______ her pen.

Finished?
Page 101, Puzzle 11A

Over to you!

5 **Draw two pictures of actions. Use the verbs below.**

run dance swim sing
drop fall push

Can the class guess the action?

Student A: He's swimming.
Student B: Correct! / Incorrect!

Building the topic

Vocabulary

1 Look at the picture. Label the rooms with the words below.

living room kitchen bathroom
dining room bedroom yard

Now listen and repeat.

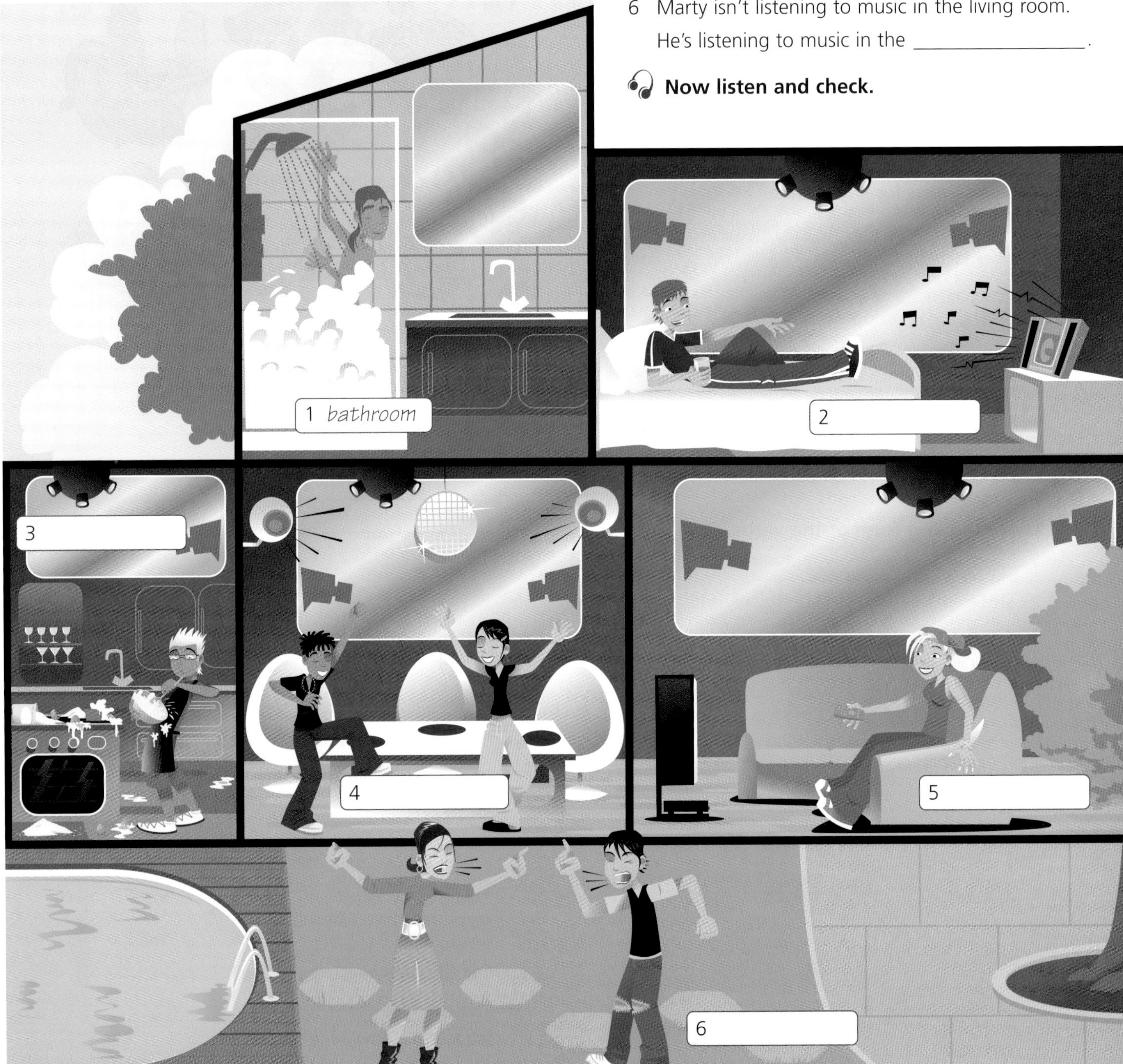

2 Fill in the blanks with the words from exercise 1.

1 Melanie isn't watching TV in the kitchen. She's watching TV in the *living room*.
2 Lara and Julio aren't dancing in the yard. They're dancing in the ________.
3 Pedro isn't making a cake in the bathroom. He's making a cake in the ________.
4 David and Jasmin aren't shouting in the dining room. They're shouting in the ________.
5 Paul isn't singing in the bedroom. He's singing in the ________.
6 Marty isn't listening to music in the living room. He's listening to music in the ________.

Now listen and check.

Grammar

Present progressive (negative)

Talking about now

1 Look at the chart.

Negative		
I'm	**not**	watch**ing** TV.
You	**aren't**	read**ing**.
He / She / It	**isn't**	sing**ing**.
We	**aren't**	listen**ing** to music.
You	**aren't**	mak**ing** a cake.
They	**aren't**	danc**ing**.

2 Look at picture A. Write sentences with the words in parentheses.

1 The singer *is singing* . (sing)
2 The guitarist ________________ the guitar. (play)
3 A woman ________________ a book. (read)
4 Two boys ________________ a ball. (throw)
5 Two girls ________________ soda. (drink)
6 A girl ________________ . (dance)

3 Look at picture B. Write sentences to compare with picture A.

1 The singer *isn't singing* . *He's dancing* .
2 The guitarist ________________ .
________________ .
3 A woman ________________ .
________________ .
4 Two boys ________________ .
________________ .
5 Two girls ________________ .
________________ .
6 A girl ________________ .
________________ .

Finished?
Page 101, Puzzle 11B

Over to you!

4 Make the sentences true for you.

1 My teacher is skiing right now.
My teacher isn't skiing. She's teaching English.
2 My mom is dancing.
3 My friend is singing.
4 My cousins are having breakfast.
5 My dad is ice-skating.
6 My brother / sister is riding a bike.

Living English

A day in the life ...

Jo Ross is a young pop star. She lives with her friends, Pedro and Angela. Today she's getting ready for a TV show.

1 It's six o'clock in the morning. Jo is having breakfast. She's very tired. Pedro is talking on the phone and Angela is watching TV.

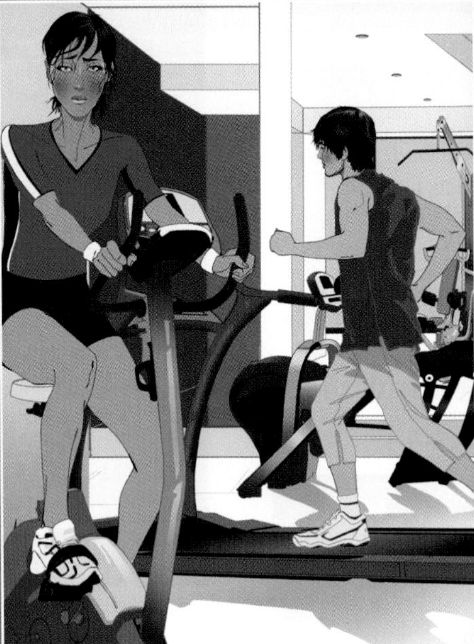

2 It's eight o'clock and Jo and Pedro are at the gym. Jo is cycling and Pedro is running.

3 It's ten o'clock. Jo is talking on the radio. The DJ is interviewing Jo.

4 It's two o'clock in the afternoon. Jo is at the dance studio. She's practicing for the show tonight. Her teacher is shouting because Jo can't dance!

5 It's four o'clock and Jo and Angela are at the mall. Jo is buying a new dress for the show tonight.

6 It's eight o'clock and Jo is singing on the TV show "Top Idol". She is happy.

7 It's ten o'clock. Jo is having dinner, Angela is reading a magazine and Pedro is writing an e-mail. Jo is tired, but happy.

Reading

1 Read the text. What is Jo's job? Who are Pedro and Angela?

2 Read again. Fill in the chart.

Time	Person	Activity
6 a.m.	Jo	is (1) *having breakfast*.
6 a.m.	(2) ______	is watching TV.
8 a.m.	Pedro	is (3) ______________.
10 a.m.	The DJ	is (4) ______________.

Time	Person	Activity
2 p.m.	Jo	is (5) ______________.
4 p.m.	(6) ______	is buying a new dress.
8 p.m.	Jo	is (7) ______________.
10 p.m.	(8) ______	is reading a magazine.

Writing

1 Look at the Writing skills box.

Writing skills

Informal letters

We start the letter with:

Dear ______ ,

We finish the letter with:

Love, ____ **or** Write soon, ___ .

2 Read the letter from Jo to her family. How does she finish the letter?

Dear Mom and Dad,

I'm in my bedroom now. I'm writing this letter and watching a music video.

I live with two friends, Angela and Pedro. Right now, Angela is singing and dancing and Pedro is talking on the phone.

How are you?

Love,

Jo

3 Fill in the chart with information about Jo.

	Jo	You
Part of the house	*bedroom*	
Right now	*I'm writing a letter and* ______ ______	
	Angela is singing and ______ ______	
	Pedro is ______ ______	

4 Now fill in the chart with your information.

5 Write a letter. Use the text and the chart to help you.

Speaking

1 Listen and read.

Who's that?
That's my brother. He's thirteen. He's eating a hamburger.

Who's that?
That's my sister. She's six. She's ice-skating.

2 Look at the Pronunciation box. Listen to the examples.

Pronunciation

'th' sounds

th **has two different sounds.**

/ð/ /θ/

that **th**irteen

Listen again and repeat.

3 Listen. Put the words in the correct column.

brother thirsty thirty the

/ð/	/θ/
brother	

4 Practice the dialog with your partner.

5 Draw a picture of someone in your family. Change the words in blue. Write a new dialog. Now practice the dialog in class.

12 Right now

Grammar: present progressive (*yes / no questions*); present progressive (*wh-* questions)
Vocabulary: actions; clothes

Exploring the topic

Follow the Money part 1

Vocabulary

1 Match the verbs with the pictures. Write the correct number next to the words.

[3] make a phone call	[ ] shake hands
[ ] follow	[ ] exchange
[ ] wave	[ ] carry

Now listen and repeat.

2 Read and listen to the story. Write D (Daniels), L (Lee), S (suspect) or W (woman).

1 He is following a man. D
2 He is carrying a briefcase. ___
3 She is talking to Daniels. ___
4 They are shaking hands. ___ and ___
5 She is carrying a briefcase. ___
6 They are exchanging briefcases. ___ and ___

Grammar

Present progressive (*yes / no* questions)

Asking about now

1 Look at the chart.

Question	Short answers
Am I wav**ing**?	Yes, I **am**. / No, I**'m not**.
Are you carry**ing** a bag?	Yes, you **are**. / No, you **aren't**.
Is he / she / it mak**ing** a phone call?	Yes, he / she / it **is**. / No, he / she / it **isn't**.
Are we follow**ing** the man?	Yes, we **are**. / No, we **aren't**.
Are you exchang**ing** briefcases?	Yes, you **are**. / No, you **aren't**.
Are they shak**ing** hands?	Yes, they **are**. / No, they **aren't**.

2 Match the questions with the answers.

1 Are you reading a book? *D*
2 Is he playing computer games? ___
3 Are they making a cake? ___
4 Is she writing a letter? ___
5 Are we going to the mall? ___

A No, she isn't. She's writing an email.
B Yes, they are. It's for my birthday.
C No, we aren't. We're going to the movies.
D Yes, I am. It's a science fiction book.
E No, he isn't. He's surfing the Internet.

3 Write the questions and answers.

1 *Is she reading a book*?
No, she isn't. She's reading a magazine.

2 ____________
____________?
____
____________.

3 ____________
____________?
____
____________.

4 ____________
____________?
____
____________ a cake.

5 ____________
____________?
____
____________ the Net.

6 ____________
____________?
____
____________.

Finished?
Page 102, Puzzle 12A

Over to you!

4 Choose one of the actions and mime it to the class. Can the class guess the action?

eating reading drinking waving
watching playing running jumping

Student A: Are you eating?
Student B: No, I'm not.
Student C: Are you reading?
Student B: Yes, I am.

Building the topic

Vocabulary

1 Label the pictures with the words below.

pants boots shirt jacket skirt glasses
sunglasses shoes

Now listen and repeat.

2 Read and listen to the dialog .
Now choose the correct picture: A or B.

3 Look at the pictures. Fill in the blanks with the correct word from exercise 1.

1 Woman A is wearing black *pants*.
2 Woman B is wearing brown __________.
3 Woman B is wearing a blue __________.
4 Woman A is wearing a red __________.
5 Woman B is wearing a red __________.

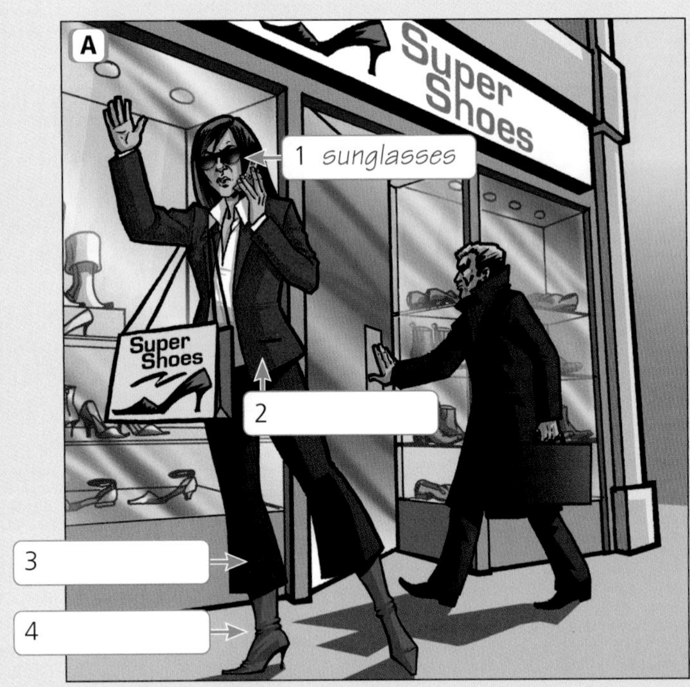

Follow the Money part 2

In a shopping mall. Agent Daniels and Agent Lee are talking on cell phones. They are in different locations in the shopping mall.

Lee: Daniels? Are we looking for the suspect?

Daniels: Yes, we are. And we're looking for the suspect's friend.

Lee: Why are we looking for her?

Daniels: You know! Because she has a briefcase. Wait! I see her!

Lee: OK. What's she wearing?

Daniels: She's wearing black pants, a white shirt, a red jacket and green boots. And she's wearing big sunglasses.

Lee: OK. What is she carrying?

Daniels: Oh no! She isn't carrying the briefcase! She's carrying a big shopping bag from "Super Shoes".

Lee: What is she doing, Daniels?

Daniels: She's talking on her cell phone. And she's waving.

Lee: Daniels! You idiot! It's me!

Daniels: Oh! Sorry! So where is the woman with the briefcase?

Lee: I don't know, Daniels. But the suspect is next to me. He's carrying a black briefcase. Come here, now!

Grammar

Present progressive (*wh*- questions)

Asking about now

Finished?
Page 102, Puzzle 12B

1 **Look at the chart.**

Questions			
What	**am**	I	do**ing**?
What	**are**	you	carry**ing**?
Where	**is**	he / she / it	go**ing**?
What	**are**	we	wear**ing**?
Why	**are**	you	follow**ing** the man?
What	**are**	they	do**ing**?

2 **Put the words in the correct order to make questions.**

1 are / What / reading / you
What are you reading ?
2 celebrating / they / Why / are
______________________________?
3 David / wearing / What / is
______________________________?
4 carrying / they / are / What
______________________________?
5 is / Why / waving / she
______________________________?

3 **Jane and her friend are talking on the phone. Write the questions.**

Hi, Jane. (1) *What are you doing* ? (you / do)
I'm reading a book.
(2) ______________________? (you / read)
It's the new Harry Potter book.
(3) ______________________? (you / sit)
I'm in the living room.
(4) ______________________? (Tim / do)
He's watching '*Follow the Money*' on TV.
(5) __________________ that? (he / watch)
Because he likes it, I guess.
(6) ______________________?
(your mom and dad / do)
They're making a pizza.
Yum! I'm coming to your house for dinner!

Over to you!

4 **Look at the picture below . Ask and answer in class. Can the class guess the person?**

Student A: Is the person throwing a ball?
Student B: Yes, he is.
Student A: Is he wearing a blue shirt?
Student B: No, he isn't.
Student A: Is he Barry?
Student B: Yes, he is!

Living English

Review

You need a dice and counters.
Throw the dice.
Answer correctly – go forward!
Answer incorrectly – go back!
START
1
Ask another player his / her name and age.
Is your question correct? Go to 4
Is your question incorrect? Go to START
2
Complete the sentence "My birthday is in ... "
Correct? Go to 4
Incorrect? Go to START
11
12
Complete the sentences about your city or country. "There's a ..." and "There are ..."
Correct? Go to 15
Incorrect? Go to 10
13
Complete the sentences "I get up at ..." and "I go to school at ..."
Correct? Go to 15
Incorrect? Go to 4
14
Ask another player "Do you ...?"
Is your question correct?Go to 15
Is your question incorrect? Go to 10
15
16
Complete the sentences "I have _____ eyes" and "I have _____ hair"
Correct? Go to 20
Incorrect? Go to 10
17
Take an extra turn!
Complete the sentences "I like ..." and "I don't like ..."
Correct? Go to 20
Incorrect? Go to 15

3
Take an extra turn!
4
5
Say four months.
Correct? Go to 10.
Incorrect? Go to 4
6
Say four jobs.
Correct? Go to 10.
Incorrect? Go to 4
7
Go back to Start!
8
Name four sports.
Correct? Go to 15
Incorrect? Go to START
9
Say four things in a house.
Correct? Go to 15
Incorrect? Go to 4
10
19
Ask another player "How often do you...?
Is your question correct? Go to 20
Is your question incorrect? Go to 15
20
FINISH

Review 6

Vocabulary

Actions

1 Find eight verbs in the word snake.

Rooms

2 Label the pictures with the names of the rooms.

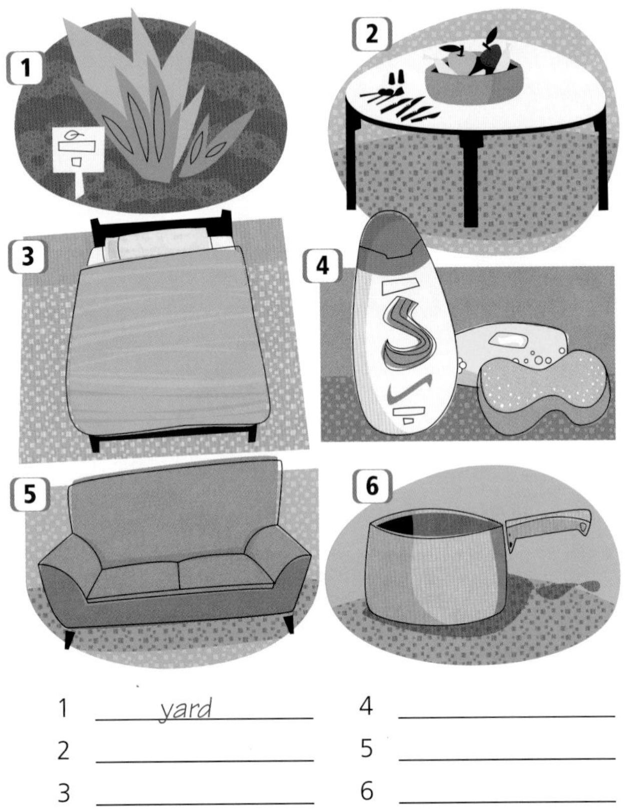

1 *yard*
2 ________
3 ________
4 ________
5 ________
6 ________

Actions

3 Fill in the blanks with the missing vowels (a, e, i, o, or u).

1 w *a* v *e*
2 __ x c h __ n g __
3 s h __ k __ h __ n d s
4 m __ k __ __ p h __ n __ c __ ll
5 f __ l l __ w
6 c __ r r y

Clothes

4 Label the pictures.

1 *sunglasses*
2 ________
3 ________
4 ________
5 ________
6 ________
7 ________
8 ________

Grammar

Present progressive (affirmative and negative)

1 Look at the pictures. Write sentences with the words in parentheses.

1 (Brett / watch TV / play computer games)
Brett isn't watching TV.
He's playing computer games.

2 (Suki / read a book / look at a photo album)
________.
________.

3 (James and Anna / eat cake / eat ice cream)
________.
________.

4 (Alex / ice-skate / surf)
________.
________.

5 (Sam and Jo / play basketball / play soccer)
________.
____

Present progressive (*yes / no* questions)

2 **Jack is talking to his mom on the phone. Complete the questions and short answers. Use the words in parentheses.**

Mom: Hi, Jack (1) _Are you sitting on the beach_ ? (you / sit)

Jack: Yes, (2) ________________. My friends are playing volleyball.

Mom: (3) ________________ volleyball? (Bret / play)

Jack: (4) No, ________________. He's playing computer games.

Mom: (5) ________________________________? (James and Ana / play computer games)

Jack: No, (6) ________________. They're eating ice creams.

Mom: ________________________________ too? (Suki / eat ice creams)

Jack: No, (8) ________________. She's reading a magazine. OK, see you next week, Mom!

3 **Complete the questions. Use the words in parentheses.**

1 _Why is she shouting_ ?
(Why / she / shout) Because she's angry.

2 ________________________________?
(Where / you / go) To Las Vegas.

3 ________________________________?
(What / they / do) They're having dinner.

4 ________________________________?
(What / she / wear) A green jacket.

5 ________________________________?
(What / he / carry) A blue bag.

6 ________________________________?
(Why / I / laugh) Because the movie is funny.

Study skills

Self assessment

When you finish a unit, make a list of what you can do.

1 **Look at your work in unit 11. Write a check (✓) next to the things you can do from this list.**

1 I can change verbs into the *-ing* form.
2 I can make the affirmative form of the present progressive.
3 I can say the rooms in a house.
4 I can make the negative form of the present progressive.
5 I can write about what people are doing right now.
6 I can talk about what people are doing right now.
7 I can describe a picture in the present progressive.
8 I can write an informal letter.
9 I can pronounce words with *th*.
10 I can talk about people in my family.

2 **What things from the list do you need to practice? How can you practice them?**

engage

PUZZLE 1A

BREAK THE CODE

a = * **e** = & **i** = >
o = @ **u** = %

Dr&w B*rrym@r& >s fr@m C*l>f@rn>*

R@n*ld>nh@ >s fr@m P@rt@ *l&gr&

PUZZLE 1B

Unscramble the message from Ivan.

HI. 'S .WR N ME' YOU MY HAT AME NA S I? VAN

HI. ___ ___ ___ ___
VAN ___ ___ ___ ___
___ ___ ?__

PUZZLE 2A

Break the code and write the sentence.

A	B	C	D	E	F	G	H	I	J	K	L	M
8				6				16				

N	O	P	Q	R	S	T	U	V	W	X	Y	Z

I'_ _ _ _ A _ I _ E _ I _ _ _ E _.
16 20 15 13 4 8 1 16 14 6 1 16 21 11 4 6 14

I'_ A _ _ _ _ E _ _!
16 20 8 2 4 12 18 6 15 4

PUZZLE 2B

Circle ten adjectives (→ or ↓) in the wordsearch.

D	C	T	R	Y	I	K	S	O
T	H	I	R	S	T	Y	S	H
W	C	R	W	A	M	U	C	U
W	E	E	B	D	C	H	A	N
Z	N	D	W	H	E	O	R	G
A	N	G	R	Y	I	T	E	R
M	C	O	L	D	Z	N	D	Y
Q	T	P	H	A	P	P	Y	S
J	B	O	R	E	D	M	A	K

PUZZLE 3A

Unscramble the words. Use the letters in the boxes to make the last word.

WNE	N E W
THROS	_ _ _ _ _
NOGL	_ _ _ _
GIB	_ _ _
PAHCE	_ _ _ _ _
MLSLA	_ _ _ _ _
LOD	_ _ _
	_ _ _ U _ _ _

PUZZLE 3B

Brain Teaser.

Who is Tom's Mother

- Delia isn't Tom's sister.
- Carol isn't Tom's mother.
- Delia is Carol's mother.
- Tom isn't Delia's brother.
- Carol is Tom's sister.

Reading for FUN

Lucy ★ Liu

Star Profile

Name:	Lucy Liu.
Date of birth:	December 2nd, 1968.
Nationality:	She's from New York, the United States.
Family:	Her parents are from China. Lucy is not married.

project

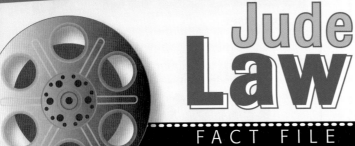

Jude Law

FACT FILE

1 Read the profile. Match the words to the information.

Job Family Date of birth
Nationality ~~Name~~

Name : His name is Jude Law.

_____________ : He's British. He's from London, United Kingdom.

_____________ : His date of birth is December 29th, 1972.

_____________ : He's an actor. His famous movies are Sky Captain and Aviator.

_____________ : His dad is Peter and his mom is Maggie. They are teachers. His sister's name is Natasha. She's a photographer.

2 Now choose a famous person.

3 Find a photo and information. (name, nationality etc)

4 Write a profile. Use the profile above as a model.

engage

PUZZLE 4A

Find the following objects. How many are there?

There are three *computers* .

There are four ________ .

There are five ________ .

There are six ________ .

There are seven ________ .

There are eight ________ .

PUZZLE 4B

Break the code. Where's the sports store?

A	B	C	D	E	F	G	H	I	J	K	L	M	N	O	P	Q	R	S	T	U	V	W	X	Y	Z
				12										19											

_ _ E	_ _ O _ _ _	_ _ O _ E	_ _	_ _ _ O _ _	_ _ O _	_ _ E	_ O _ _ E	_ _ E _ _ E _.
11 2 12	16 6 19 7 11 16	16 11 19 7 12	2 16	14 5 7 19 16 16	1 7 19 18	11 3 12	18 19 24 2 12	11 3 12 14 11 12 7

PUZZLE 5A

Solve the puzzle. What is Jack's birthday present?

Hi! I'm Jack.

1. This is my...
2. That is my...
3. These are my...
4. That is my...
5. This is my...
6. These are my...
7. Those are my...

My birthday present is two...

PUZZLE 5B

Find the words. Use the other letters to make the secret message.

S	R	E	T	S	O	P	T	S	H
S	E	E	T	R	E	S	S	E	A
S	T	S	U	R	E	P	E	S	I
S	U	E	S	H	M	N	D	A	E
B	E	D	S	A	B	R	Y	C	O
U	R	I	L	O	L	D	E	K	S
K	D	O	X	Z	L	G	O	O	Z
C	O	E	X	A	U	C	C	O	O
F	S	T	S	L	U	X	Y	B	W
I	Y	Z	K	D	Q	A	M	R	B

~~BEDS~~ BOOKCASES BOXES CLOSETS DISHES GLASSES LAMPS POSTERS

THE _ _ _ _ _ _ _ _ _ _ _ _

_ _ _ _ _ _ _ _ _ _ _ _ _ _

PUZZLE 6A

What can Maria do? What can't she do? Unscramble the message.

FA	SHE	CA	'T	N J
HE	ST.	UMP	RUN	CAN
BU	T S	HI	GH.	
SHE				

PUZZLE 6B

What's the sport?

BGUYR R U G B Y

FSIUGRN _ _ _ _ _ _ _

AABKTLBELS _ _ _ _ _ _ _ _ _ _

NTISEN _ _ _ _ _ _

RCESCO _ _ _ _ _ _

MGWIINSM _ _ _ _ _ _ _ _

Reading for FUN

New Zealand

New Zealand is a beautiful country in the Pacific Ocean. There are beautiful animals, beaches, big volcanoes, lakes, rivers and beaches.

It's a cool place to visit. You can do many activities there. You can go bungee jumping, skydiving, and mountain climbing.

Facts about New Zealand

- *There are fourteen National Parks in New Zealand.*
- *There are about four million people in New Zealand.*
- *Rugby is very popular in New Zealand. Their team is called the All Blacks.*
- *The places in the Lord of the Rings movies are in New Zealand.*

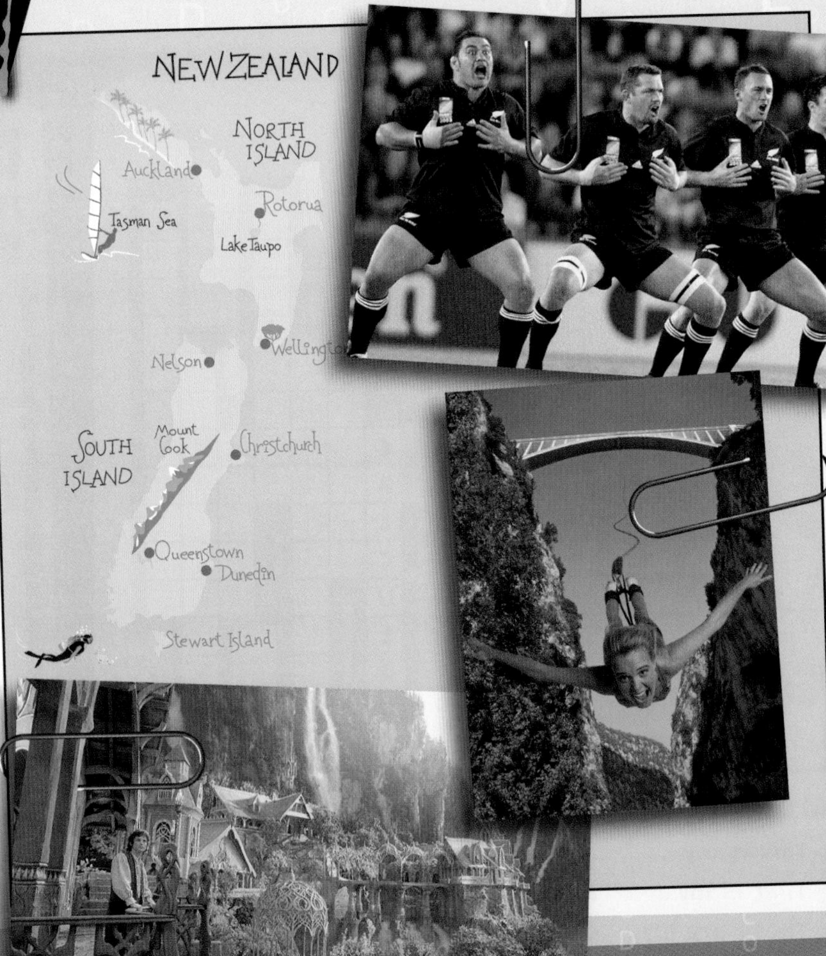

Project

American Football

1 Read the profile. Put the words in the correct place.

Rules Where? Favorites
~~Introduction~~ Players

Introduction : American football is from the United States. It is 128 years old.

__________________ On a field.

__________________ There are eleven players in a team.

__________________ Kick the ball. Throw the ball. Pass the ball.

__________________ My favorite player is Todd Johnson. His team is the Chicago Bears.

helmet
shoulder pad
jersey
football
knee pad

2 Now choose a sport.

3 Draw a picture or find a photo. Find information about the sport. (where?, how old?, equipment, how to play, your favorite player and team)

4 Write your sport profile. Use the profile above as a model.

5 Put your descriptions in a class magazine about sport. Read the other students' descriptions.

engage

PUZZLE 7A

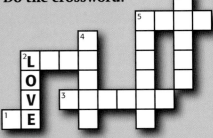

How many verbs can you make?

1. *go*

n h r e y w h r w s a c e t a l i t a d a e p k t t a g l f i i o v

PUZZLE 7B

Do the crossword.

2 L O V E

Across

1. .... reads books.
2. I .... in New York City.
3. She .... school at 8.30 in the morning.
5. They .... soccer at school.

Down

2. "I .... Brazil. It's really beautiful!"
4. He .... his friends at the mall.
5. Monica .... beautiful pictures.
6. We .... TV in the evening.

PUZZLE 8A

What do Greg and Jenny do?

REGG — G R E G (8)
SOEND'T (1)
CRSUEE
OLPPEE
HE
SEOND'T (5)
MIBCL
NANMIUSOT
NEYNJ (4)
SEDNO'T
WINTERVEI (6)
EOLPEP (3)
HES
NOEDS'T (7)
KATE
HOSPOT (2)

1 2 3 4   5 6 7 8 !

PUZZLE 8B

Who is who? Write the name under the picture. Follow the lines. Who rescues the girl?

Matt the Marvellous has dark, curly hair. He doesn't have long hair. He has blue eyes.

Fantastic Fred has green eyes. He has long, dark hair. He doesn't have curly hair.

Superboy has short, blond hair. He doesn't have straight hair or green eyes. He has brown eyes.

PUZZLE 9A

Do the puzzle. What's the mystery word?

1. Do we dance at the *dance club*? Yes, we, do.
2. Does she play sports at the ______ ____? Yes, she does.
3. Do they go to the beach on vacation? No, they don't. They go to the _______.
4. Do you surf at the _____? Yes, I do.
5. Do you enjoy going to the _____ ____? No, I don't. It's scary.
6. Does he play at the ______ ____? No, he doesn't. He watches the game.
7. Do you go to _______? Yes, we do.

1 DANCECLUB
2
3
4
5
6
7

G	N	D	P	M	B	M	C	C	A	Y	W	S	U	X
R	O	M	A	N	T	I	C	X	C	T	S	C	N	P
H	E	M	R	O	N	T	D	Y	T	N	S	I	W	G
J	E	I	A	M	A	S	R	O	I	Y	B	E	Q	X
H	N	A	V	N	J	O	C	D	O	A	F	N	M	H
G	E	X	C	I	T	I	N	G	N	K	E	C	K	H
H	R	Y	S	S	N	I	K	S	E	R	L	E	Z	Z
J	N	O	E	R	B	T	C	C	Y	X	T	F	W	Z
V	S	V	R	W	P	O	B	A	M	C	F	I	R	Z
N	O	L	A	R	G	H	O	R	R	O	R	C	E	B
L	O	V	E	S	T	O	R	Y	V	W	U	T	D	O
R	A	D	Y	W	S	H	E	O	I	E	J	I	X	R
U	X	D	L	N	Q	N	S	R	N	B	R	O	K	I
H	P	F	C	Y	A	F	U	N	N	Y	G	N	V	N
C	O	M	E	D	Y	B	P	C	H	Q	H	Y	Z	G

PUZZLE 9B

Circle the words (→ or ↓) in the wordsearch.

ACTION
BORING
COMEDY
EXCITING
FUNNY
HORROR
LOVE STORY
~~ROMANTIC~~
SCARY
SCIENCE FICTION

Reading for FUN

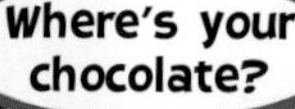

project

Imagine a life

1 Look at the photo and read the text. Put the words in the correct place.

Hobbies Appearance

Family ~~Personal information~~

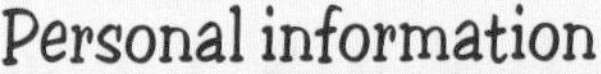

Personal information

Her name is Monique and she's twenty-eight. She's from Malaysia, but she lives in Los Angeles. She's a TV host. She interviews people for a TV show about sports.

____

She has long dark hair and brown eyes. She's tall.

____

On the weekend, Monique goes to concerts. She likes pop music because it's awesome. She also surfs. She likes it because it's exciting.

____

Monique has two brothers and a sister. She has a boyfriend. His name is Raphael and he's from Italy.

2 Now choose a photo, or find your own photo.

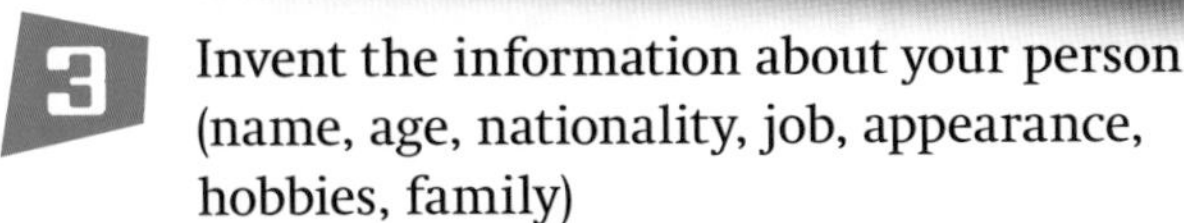

3 Invent the information about your person. (name, age, nationality, job, appearance, hobbies, family)

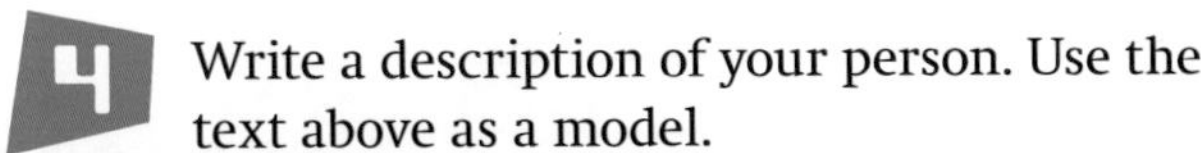

4 Write a description of your person. Use the text above as a model.

engage

PUZZLE 10A

Do the crossword.

Across

1 Before the party, we .... the room with balloons.

2 We give a .... for our parents. We play musical instruments and sing.

4 Our classroom is small, so we have the party in a big ....

6 We give .... to our friends and teachers.

Down

1 At the party, we sing and ....

3 All the kids wear nice .... to the party.

5 We .... cake at the party.

PUZZLE 10B

Fill in the blanks and find your way out!

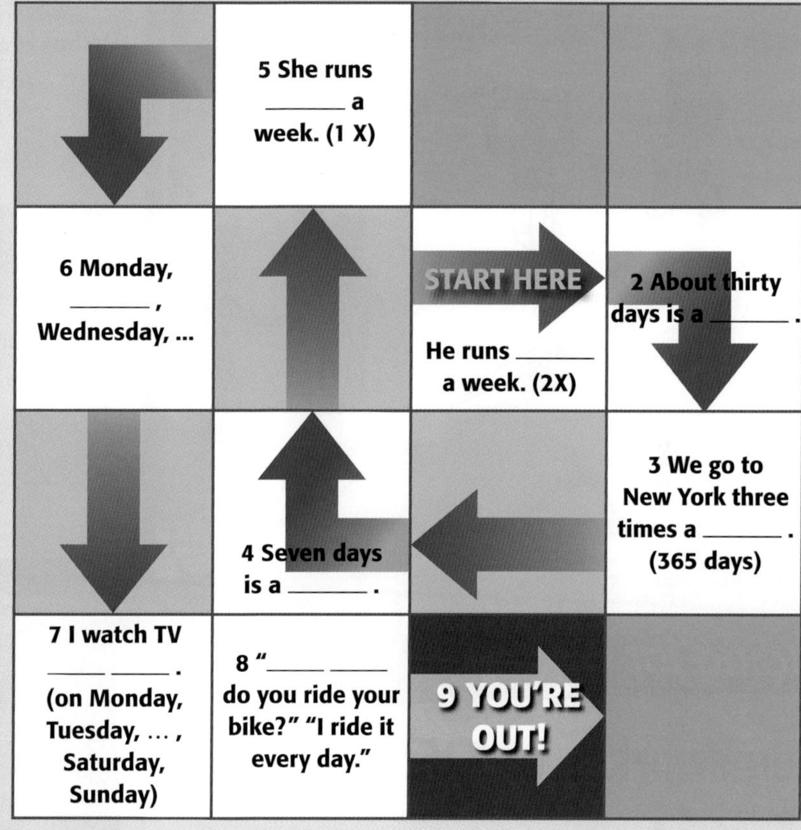

5 She runs ______ a week. (1 X)
6 Monday, ______ , Wednesday, ...
START HERE
He runs ______ a week. (2X)
2 About thirty days is a ______ .
3 We go to New York three times a ______ . (365 days)
4 Seven days is a ______ .
7 I watch TV ____ ____ . (on Monday, Tuesday, ... , Saturday, Sunday)
8 "____ ____ do you ride your bike?" "I ride it every day."
9 YOU'RE OUT!

PUZZLE 11A

Put the words in bold into the crossword. Which word is extra?

I am **opening** a window.

Tina and Paul are **laughing** at the television.

He is **closing** the door.

Jon is **pulling** my hair.

Be careful! You are **dropping** that plate!

They are **shouting** at the soccer game.

Hannah is **falling**.

Jon is **pushing** Hannah.

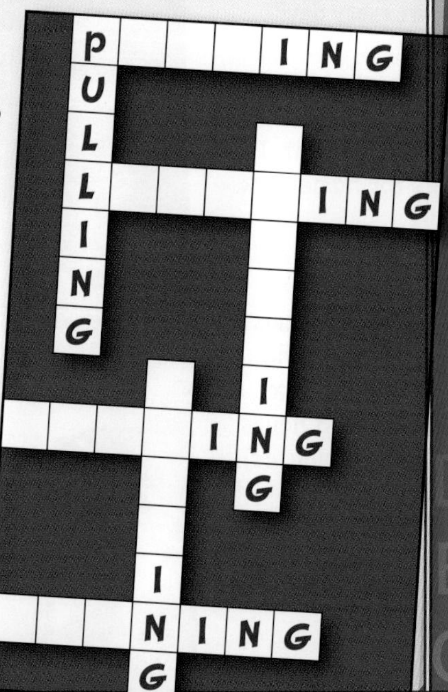

PUZZLE 11B

Look at the clues and unscramble the letters to find out where Sarah is...

1 She isn't watching TV. (ivnlig moro)
She isn't in the l i v i n g r o o m.

2 She isn't having a shower. (mtoabhro)
She isn't in the _ _ _ _ _ _ _ _.

3 She isn't making a cake. (ckihetn)
She isn't in the _ _ _ _ _ _ _.

4 She isn't sleeping. (domeobr)
She isn't in the _ _ _ _ _ _ _.

5 She isn't playing soccer. (drya)
She isn't in the _ _ _ _.

Sarah is in the _ _ _ _ _ _ _ _ _ _.

PUZZLE 12A

Read the clues and label the people.

Will and Alison aren't waving.
David isn't making a phone call.
Sabrina isn't waving.
Jennifer and Melissa aren't shaking hands.
Victoria isn't carrying a letter.

PUZZLE 12B

There is an extra word in each question. Find the extra words and make another question with them.

What is John ~~am~~ doing?
Where are they going why?
Where is doing Pam going?
How are they decorating I the room?
What are you this watching on TV?

___ ___ ___ ___ ___ ___ t h i s ?

What word is it?
It has five letters.
The first and last letters are the same.
The second letter looks like nothing.
The other two letters are the answer to this question:
Denzel is ___ ___ his room.

The word is ___ ___ ___ ___ ___

Reading for FUN

Homework ... or TV?

Some 13-year-olds in different countries answer two questions:

1. Do you watch TV for more than 2 hours every day?
2. Do you do your homework for more than 2 hours every day?

In Scotland, 90% say yes for watching TV, but only 14% say yes for doing homework! In the United States it's 84% for TV, and 29% for homework. In some countries it's different. In France, 49% say yes for TV, but 55% say yes for homework. In China, it's 35% for TV, 44% for homework.

How much TV do you watch?

The answer is different in different places. In Japan, most people watch TV for 4 hours and 29 minutes a day. In the United States, it's 4 hours and 25 minutes. Europe is next, with 3 hours and 33 minutes, then the Middle East (3 hours and 15 minutes) and Latin America (3 hours and 14 minutes).

What shows do you like?

About 50% of people around the world like dramas, especially police shows. Music and game shows are popular in Europe and Latin America. Reality TV is popular everywhere.

project

TV watching habits in the United States

The Questions

1. What kind of shows do you like?
2. What kind of shows don't you like?
3. What are your favorite shows?
4. Do you have a TV in your bedroom?
5. How many TVs do you have in your house?
6. Do you watch TV and have dinner at the same time?
7. How many hours of TV do you watch every day?

The Results

- Young people in the United States watch more than 4 hours of television every day.
- 40% of kids watch TV and have dinner at the same time.
- 56% have a TV in their bedrooms.
- 35% of houses have two TVs. 41% have three or more TVs.
- Kids like dramas, comedies and music shows.
- Their favorite shows are the Simpsons, American Idol, Will and Grace, and the O.C.
- They don't like science and nature shows, or news programs.

1 Read the survey above. Match the questions with the answers.

2 Work in groups of five. Ask and answer the questions from the survey above.

Question

How many hours of TV do you watch every day?

3 2.5 4 3 3

Do you watch TV and have dinner at the same time?

Yes No No Yes No

3 Write a report about your group's TV watching habits.

TV watching habits

60% of our group watch three hours of television every day.

20% watch four hours a day, and 20% watch two and a half hours.

4 Share your results with the class. Do you have the same or different results?

Grammar summary

Unit 1

be (affirmative)

Affirmative	
Long form	Short form
I am Akiro.	**I'm** Akiro.
You are thirteen.	**You're** thirteen.
He is eleven.	**He's** eleven.
She is fourteen.	**She's** fourteen.
It is a country.	**It's** a country.
We are in class.	**We're** in class.
You are from Japan.	**You're** from Japan.
They are e-pals.	**They're** e-pals.

We can use *be* for name, age and nationality.
I'm Maria, I'm twelve, and I'm from Spain.

be (questions)

Questions	Answers
What's your **name**?	I'm Vera. / My name's Vera.
Where are you **from**?	I'm from Brazil. / I'm Brazilian.
How old are you?	I'm 14 years old.

We can use *be* (questions) to ask about name, age and nationality.
Where is Sara from? Sara is from Mexico.

Unit 2

a / an

We use *a* before words that begin with a consonant.
a student, a teacher, a firefighter, a desk

We use *an* before words that begin with a vowel.
an actor, an artist, an apple, an orange

We use *a / an* with jobs.
I'm a soccer player.

We don't use *a / an* with plural nouns.
We're teachers. (NOT ~~We're a teachers.~~)

be (negative)

Negative					
Long form			Short form		
I	**am not**	an actor.	I	**'m not**	an actor.
You	**are not**	an artist.	You	**aren't**	an artist.
He / She / It	**is not**	a doctor.	He / She / It	**isn't**	a doctor.
We	**are not**	models.	We	**aren't**	models.
You	**are not**	singers.	You	**aren't**	singers.
They	**are not**	models.	They	**aren't**	models.

We use *not* to make *be* (negative).
I'm not fifteen. We aren't from Canada.

be + adjective

Affirmative		Negative	
I am	happy.	**I'm not**	happy.
You are	thirsty.	**You aren't**	thirsty.
He / She / It is	angry.	**He / She / It isn't**	angry.
We are	bored.	**We aren't**	bored.
You are	hungry.	**You aren't**	hungry.
They are	hot.	**They aren't**	hot.

We can use *be* to talk about feelings.
We are hungry.

Adjectives don't change with plurals.
I'm happy. We're happy. (NOT ~~We're happys~~.)

Unit 3

Possessive adjectives

Subject pronoun	Possessive adjective
I am Sara.	**My** computer is new.
You are Zoe.	**Your** skateboard is long.
He is Juan.	**His** CD player is big.
She is Dana.	**Her** phone is cheap.
It is a computer.	**Its** price is $40.
We are friends.	**Our** phones are small.
You are friends.	**Your** computer is new.
They are friends.	**Their** phones are cheap.

We use possessive adjectives to talk about possessions.
We don't use *the* with possessive adjectives.
It's my bag. (NOT ~~It's the my bag.~~)

Possessive 's

We use *'s* to talk about possessions with names.
She is Mary's sister.

be (*yes / no* questions and short answers)

Question			Short answers
Am	**I**	right?	Yes, **I am**. / No, **I'm not**.
Are	**you**	Dave?	Yes, **you are**. / No, **you aren't**.
Is	**he**	your father?	Yes, **he is**. / No, **he isn't**.
Is	**she**	your mother?	Yes, **she is**. / No, **she isn't**.
Is	**it**	your house?	Yes, **it is**. / No, **it isn't**.
Are	**we**	friends?	Yes, **we are**. / No, **we aren't**.
Are	**you**	brothers?	Yes, **you are**. / No, **you aren't**.
Are	**they**	five?	Yes, **they are**. / No, **they aren't**.

We form *yes / no* questions with *be* + subject.
They are happy. ➔ *Are they happy?*

Unit 4

Plural nouns

We add *-s* to form plurals.
mountain ➔ *mountains*
But for some plural nouns we add *-es*.
beach ➔ *beaches* *watch* ➔ *watches*
See Unit 5 Plurals (below) for more information.

there is / there are

Affirmative	
Singular	Plural
There is / **There's** a river.	**There are** mountains.
Questions and answers	
Singular	Plural
Is there a city in Patagonia?	**Are there** any penguins?
Yes, **there is**. No, **there isn't**.	Yes, **there are**. / No, **there aren't**.

We use *There is* + *a / an* with singular nouns.
There's a lake in my country.

We use *There are* with plural nouns.
There are beaches in Patagonia.

We use *Is there* + *a / an* ... ? with singular nouns.
Is there a mountain? Yes, there is.

We use *Are there any ... ?* with plural nouns.
Are there any tigers? No, there aren't.

Prepositions of place

Questions and answers
Where is the sports store? It's **across from** the movie theater.
Where is the take-out? It's **next to** the restrooms.
Where is the cyber café? It's **between** the movie theater and the fast food restaurant.
Where is the bus stop? It's **in front of** the shopping mall.

We use *Where is* or *Where's* to ask about position.
We use prepositions to talk about position.
See Unit 5, page 38, for more prepositions of place.

Unit 5

this / that / these / those

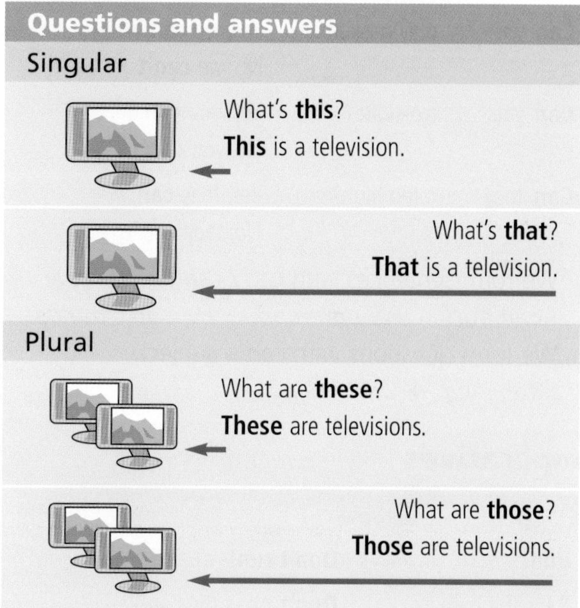

Questions and answers
Singular
What's **this**?
This is a television.
What's **that**?
That is a television.
Plural
What are **these**?
These are televisions.
What are **those**?
Those are televisions.

We use *this* and *these* for things which are near to us.
This is my cell phone. These are my books.
We use *that* and *those* for things which are not near to us.
That is her computer. Those are her pens.

Plural nouns

We add *-s* to form plurals.
one poster ➔ *two posters*

We add *-es* after *-x*, *-sh*, *-ss*, and *-ch*
one box ➔ *two boxes* *one dish* ➔ *three dishes*

Unit 6

can

Affirmative			Negative		
I	**can**	swim.	I	**can't**	swim.
You	**can**	dance.	You	**can't**	dance.
He / She / It	**can**	run fast.	He / She / It	**can't**	run fast.
We	**can**	ice-skate.	We	**can't**	ice-skate.
You	**can**	jump high.	You	**can't**	jump high.
They	**can**	ski.	They	**can't**	ski.

Questions and short answers		
Can I	swim?	Yes, I **can**. / No, I **can't**.
Can you	run fast?	Yes, you **can**. / No, you **can't**.
Can he / she / it	dance?	Yes, he / she /it **can**. / No, he / she / it **can't**.
Can we	play basketball?	Yes, we **can**. / No, we **can't**.
Can you	ice-skate?	Yes, you **can**. / No, you **can't**.
Can they	jump high?	Yes, they **can**. / No, they **can't**.

We form sentences with *can / can't* + infinitive.
I can surf. *We can read.* *He can't dance.*
We form questions with *can* + subject.
I can sing. ➔ *Can I sing?*

Imperatives

Affirmative	Negative
Run!	**Don't run**!
Pass the ball!	**Don't pass** the ball!

We use imperatives to give instructions.
Throw the ball!
We form the negative with *Don't* + verb.
Don't touch.

Unit 7

at / in

We use *at* for times of the day, and with mealtimes.
at two o' clock *at breakfast*

We use *in* with parts of the day, months, seasons and years.
in the evening *in May*
in the summer *in 2005*

Simple present (affirmative)

Affirmative		
I	**go** to school	at eight o'clock.
You	**get** up	at seven thirty.
He / She / It	**starts** school	at eight thirty.
We	**have** lunch	at twelve thirty.
You	**watch** TV	in the evening.
They	**finish** classes	at three o'clock.

We use the simple present to talk about routines and habits.
I start school at eight o'clock.

Spelling rules for simple present (*he / she / it*)

We add *-s* to the verb with *he / she / it*.
He starts school at six o'clock.

We add *-es* after *-o*, *-x*, *-sh*, and *-ch*.
He goes to the office.
It finishes at ten o'clock.
Some verbs are irregular.
She has breakfast at eight o'clock.

Unit 8

Simple present (negative)

Negative		
I	**don't**	interview people.
You	**don't**	rescue people.
He / She / It	**doesn't**	take photos.
We	**don't**	climb mountains.
You	**don't**	sing.
They	**don't**	work in an office.

We form simple present (negative) with *don't* or *doesn't*.
We don't start classes at seven o'clock.
He doesn't surf on the weekend.

In the negative, don't add *-s / -es* after *he / she / it*.
She doesn't know (NOT ~~She doesn't knows.~~)

have / has

Affirmative	Negative
I **have** short hair.	I **don't have** short hair.
You **have** long hair.	You **don't have** short hair.
He / She / It **has** blond hair.	He / She / It **doesn't have** blond hair.
We **have** curly hair.	We **don't have** curly hair.
You **have** straight hair.	You **don't have** straight hair.
They **have** wavy hair.	They **don't have** wavy hair

We use *have / has* to talk about possessions.
I have a pen. *She has a sister.*
We use *have / has* to describe people.
They have blue eyes.

In the negative, we don't use *has* with *he / she / it*.
He doesn't have a cell phone. (NOT ~~He doesn't has a cell phone.~~)

Unit 9

Simple present (*yes / no* questions)

Question			Short answers
Do	I	go to dance clubs?	Yes, I **do**. / No, I **don't**.
Do	you	go to the beach?	Yes, you **do**. / No, you **don't**.
Does	he / she / it	go to soccer games?	Yes, he / she / it **does**. / No, he / she / it **doesn't**.
Do	we	go to concerts?	Yes, we **do**. / No, we **don't**.
Do	you	go to soccer games?	Yes, you **do**. / No, you **don't**.
Do	they	go to a sports club?	Yes, they **do**. / No, they **don't**.

We form questions with *do / does* + subject + verb.
Does he know Nick? Yes, he does. / No, he doesn't.

like

Affirmative	Negative
He / She / It **likes** rap.	He / She / It **doesn't like** rap.
Question	**Answer**
Do they **like** concerts?	Yes, they **do**. / No, they **don't**.

We use *like* to talk about likes / dislikes.
We don't use *the* with like.
They like action movies. (NOT ~~They like the action movies~~).

Unit 10

Simple present (*wh-* questions)

Questions			
What	**do**	**I**	**do**?
When	**do**	**you**	**start** classes?
Why	**does**	**he / she / It**	**have** the party?
How	**do**	**we**	**go** to school?
What	**do**	**you**	**do** at the party?
Where	**do**	**they**	**have** the party?

We form simple present (*wh-* questions) with question word + *do / does* + subject + verb.
What does he do on the weekend?

Expressions of frequency

Questions and answers
How often do you go swimming? I **never** go swimming. I go swimming **twice a week**.
How often does he /she /it play a team sport? He plays a team sport **once a month**. She plays a team sport **three times a year**.

We form questions with *how often* + *do / does* + subject.
How often does Justin go to parties?

Never goes between the subject and the verb.
Justin never goes to parties (NOT ~~Justin goes to parties never.~~)

Other expressions of frequency go at the end of the sentence.
I go to concerts twice a year.

Unit 11

Present progressive (affirmative)

Affirmative	
I'**m**	dropp**ing** a glass.
You'**re**	fall**ing**.
He'**s** / She'**s** / It'**s**	push**ing** a door.
We'**re**	clos**ing** a window.
You'**re**	laugh**ing**.
They'**re**	shout**ing**.

We use the present progressive to talk about right now.
I'm eating my lunch.

We form the present progressive with subject + *be* + *-ing* form.
I'm singing.
You're relaxing.

Spelling rules for *-ing* forms

For regular verbs add *-ing*. *fall* ➔ *falling*

For verbs ending in a consonant + *-e* -~~*e*~~ + *-ing*.
close ➔ *closing* *dance* ➔ *dancing*

For verbs ending in a vowel + a consonant double the consonant + *-ing*.
drop ➔ *dropping*

Present progressive (negative)

Negative		
I'm	**not**	watch**ing** TV.
You	**aren't**	read**ing**.
He / She / It	**isn't**	sing**ing**.
We	**aren't**	listen**ing** to music.
You	**aren't**	mak**ing** a cake.
They	**aren't**	danc**ing**.

We form the present progressive (negative) with *be* + *not* + *-ing* form.
You aren't reading.

Unit 12

Present progressive (*yes* / *no* questions)

Question			Short answers
Am	I	wav**ing**?	Yes, I **am**. / No, I**'m not**.
Are	you	surf**ing**?	Yes, you **are**. / No, you **aren't**.
Is	he / she / it	cook**ing**?	Yes, he / she / it **is**. / No, he / she / it **isn't**.
Are	we	read**ing**?	Yes, we **are**. / No, we **aren't**.
Are	you	eat**ing**?	Yes, you **are**. / No, you **aren't**.
Are	they	go**ing**?	Yes, they **are**. / No, they **aren't**.

We form questions with *be* + subject + *-ing* form.
She's laughing. ➔ *Is she laughing?*

Present progressive (*wh-* questions)

Questions			
What	**am**	I	do**ing**?
What	**are**	you	carry**ing**?
Where	**is**	he / she / it	go**ing**?
What	**are**	we	wear**ing**?
Why	**are**	you	follow**ing** the man?
What	**are**	they	do**ing**?

We form questions with question word + *be* + subject + *-ing* form.
What is she doing?

Word list

Welcome

Numbers
one /wən/
two /tu/
three /θri/
four /fɔr/
five /faiv/
six /sɪks/
seven /sevən/
eight /eit/
nine /nain/
ten /ten/
eleven /ɪ'levən/
twelve /twelv/
thirteen /θər'tin/
fourteen /ˌfɔr'tin/
fifteen /ˌfɪf'tin/
sixteen /ˌsɪk'stin/
seventeen /ˌsevən'tin/
eighteen /ˌei'tin/
nineteen /ˌnain'tin/
twenty /'twenty/
thirty /'θərti/
forty /'fɔrti/
fifty /'fɪfti/
sixty /'sɪksti/
seventy /'sevənti/
eighty /'eiti/
ninety /'nainti/
one hundred /wən 'həndrɪd/

Colors
black /blæk/
blue /blu/
brown /braun/
green /grin/
orange /'ɔrindʒ/
pink /pɪŋk/
purple /'pərpəl/
red /red/
white /(h)wait/
yellow /'yelou/

Classroom objects
desk /desk/
eraser /ɪ'reisər/
notebook /noutbʊk/
pen /pen/
pencil /'pensəl/
ruler /'rulər/

Days of the week
Monday /'mʌndeɪ/
Tuesday /'tuzdeɪ/
Wednesday /'wenzdeɪ/
Thursday /'θərzdeɪ/
Friday /'fraideɪ/
Saturday /'sætərdeɪ/
Sunday /'səndeɪ/

Months of the year
January /'dzænyuˌeri/
February /'febyuˌeri, febru-/
March /martʃ/
April /'eiprəl/
May /mei/
June /dʒun/
July /dʒu'lai, dzə-/
August /'ɔgəst/
September /sep'tembər/
October /ak'toubər/
November /nou'vembər/
December /dɪ'sembər/

Unit 1

Countries
Australia /ɔs'treiliə/
Brazil /brə'zɪl/
Guatemala /gwa'təmalə /
Japan /dʒə'pæn/
Mexico /'meksɪkou/
Russia /'rəʃə/
South Africa /sauθ 'æfrikə/
Spain /spein/
The United Kingdom /ðə yu'nɪtəd 'kɪŋgdəm/
The United States /ðə yu'nɪtəd steitz/

Nationalities
American /ə'merɪkən/
Australian /ɔs'treiliən/
Brazilian /brə'zɪliən/
British /'brɪtɪʃ/
Guatemalan /gwa'təmalən/
Japanese /dʒæpə'niz/
Mexican /'meksɪkən/
Russian /'rəʃən/
South African /sauθ 'æfrikən/
Spanish /'spænɪʃ/

Living English
nickname /'nɪkˌneim/

Unit 2

Jobs
actor /'æktər/
artist /'artɪst/
doctor /'daktər/
firefighter /'faiər faitər
model /'madəl/
singer /sɪŋər/
skateboarder /skeitbɔrdər/
soccer player /'sakər pleiər/
student /'studənt/
teacher /'titʃər/

Feelings
angry /'æŋgri/
bored /bɔrd/
cold /kould/
happy /'hæpi/
hot /hat/
hungry /'həŋgri/
sad /sæd/
scared /skerd/
thirsty /θərsti/
tired /taiərd/

Unit 3

Describing objects
big /bɪg/
cheap /tʃip/
expensive /ɪk'spensɪv/
long /lɔŋ/
new /nu/
old /ould/
short /ʃaut/
small /smɔl/

Objects
bag /bæg/
CD player /ˌsi'di 'pleiər/
cell phone /sel foun/
computer /kəm'pyutər/
skateboard /'skeitbɔrd/

Family
brother /'brəðər/
father /'faðər/
grandfather /'grænˌfaðər/
grandmother /'grænˌməðər/
grandparents /'grænˌpærəntz/
mother /'məðər/
parents /'pærəntz/
sister /'sɪstər/

Unit 4

Nature

animal /'ænəməl/
beach /bitʃ/
bear /ber/
city /'sɪti/
dolphin /'dalfən/
forest /'fɔrɪst, 'farɪst/
lake /leik/
mountain /'mauntən/
panda /'pændə/
penguin /'pengwɪn/
river /'rɪvər/
seal /'siəl/
tiger /'taigər/
whale /'(h)weiəl/

Places in a town

bus stop /bəs stap/
clothes store /klouz stɔr/
cyber café /'saibər ˌkæ'fei/
fast food restaurant /fæst fud 'rɛstrɑnt, 'rɛstərɑnt/
movie theater /'muvi 'θiətər, θi'eitər/
music store /'myuzɪk stɔr/
restrooms /restrums, rʊms/
shopping mall /'ʃapɪŋ mɔl/
sports store /spɔrtz stɔr/

Prepositions of place

across from /ə'krɔs frəm/
between /bi'twin/
in front of /in frənt əv/
next to /nekst tə/

Living English

building /'bɪldɪŋ/
seat /sit/
store /stɔr/
tall /tɔl/
team /tim/
theater /'θiətər, θi'eitər/

Other

ideal /ai'diəl/

Unit 5

Objects

calculator /'kælkyeˌleitər/
camera /'kæm(ə)rə/
CD player /ˌsi'di 'pleiər/
clock /klak/
dish /dɪʃ/
game console /geim 'kanˌsoul/
glass /glæs/
stereo /'stɛrioʊ/
object /'abdʒɪkt/
radio /'reidiou/
telephone /'teləˌfoun/
television /'teləˌvɪʒən/
watch /watʃ/

Furniture

bed /bed/
bedside table /bedseid 'teibəl/
bookcase /'bʊkˌkeis/
box /baks/
chair /tʃer/
closet /'klazɪt/
desk /desk/
door /dɔr/
furniture /'fərnɪtʃər/
lamp /læmp/
poster /'poustər/
window /'wɪndou/

Prepositions

in /ɪn/
on /an/
under /'əndər/

Living English

bedroom /bedrum, -rʊm/
cave /keiv/
houseboat /hausˌbout/

Unit 6

Abilities

dance /dæns/
ice-skate /'ais skeit/
jump high /dʒəmp/
play basketball /plei 'bæskitˌbɔl/
ride a horse /raid ə hɔrs/
run fast /rən fæst/
ski /ski/
swim /swim/
ride a bike /raid ə baik/

Sports rules

hit /hɪt/
kick /kɪk/
pass /pæs/
throw /θrou/
touch /tətʃ/
walk /wɔk/

Living English

mountainboard /'mauntən bɔrd/
street luge /strit ludz/
Zorb ball /zɔrb bɔl/

Magazine 2

bungee jumping /'bəndʒi dʒəmpɪŋ/
mountain climbing /'mauntən 'klaimiŋ/
rugby /'rəgbi/
skydiving /'skaidaiviŋ/
volcano /val'keinou/

Review 3

bicycle /'baisɪkəl/
dog /dɔg/
judo /'dʒudou/
karate /kə'rati/
trash can /træʃ kæn/

Unit 7

Daily activities

do my homework /du 'mai houmwərk/
finish classes /'fɪnɪʃ klæsiz/
get up /get 'əp/
go to bed /gou tə bed/
go to school /gou tə skul/
have breakfast /hæv 'brekfəst/
have dinner /hæv 'dɪnər/
have lunch /hæv ləntʃ/
start classes /start klæsiz/
watch TV /watʃ ˌti'vi/
live /lɪv/
love /ləv/
meet /mit/
paint /peint/
read /rid/
relax /rɪ'læks/
surf /sərf/
work /wərk/

Other

hospital /'haˌspɪtəl/
pop group /pap grup/

Unit 8

Activities (work)

climb mountains /klaim 'mauntəns/
interview people /'ɪntərˌvyu 'pipəl/
rescue people /'reskyu 'pipəl/
sing /sɪŋ/
take photos /teik 'foutous/

Jobs

lifeguard /laifgard/
mountaineer /ˌmauntən'ɪr/
photographer /fə'tagrəfə/
TV host /ˌti'vi hoʊst/

Physical appearance

blond /bland/
blue /blu/
brown /braun/

curly /kərli/
dark /dark/
eyes /aiz/
green /grin/
hair /her/
long /lɔŋ/
short /ʃɔrt/
straight /streit/
tall /tɔl/
wavy /weivi/

Living English

band /bænd/
concert /'kan,sərt/
farm /farm/
fashion /'fæʃən/
regular /'regyələr/
village /'vɪlɪdʒ/

Other

office /'ɔfɪs/
opera /'aprə/

Unit 9

Places

beach /bitʃ/
concert /'kan,sərt/
country /'kəntri/
dance club /dæns kləb/
party /'parti/
soccer game /'sakər geim/
sports club /spɔrtz kləb/
theme park /θim park/

Movies and adjectives

action movie /'ækʃən 'muvi/
boring /'bɔriŋ/
comedy /'kɔmədi/
exciting /ɪk'saitɪŋ/
funny /'fəni/
horror movie /'hɔror 'muvi/
love story /'ləv stɔri/
romantic /rou'mæntɪk/
scary /'skeri/
science fiction movie /'saiyəns 'fɪkʃən 'muvi/

Living English

board games /bɔrd geimz/
rock music /'rɔk 'myuzɪk/
surf /sərf/
youth club /yuθ kləb/

Other

go to the gym /gou tə ðe dʒim/
rap music /ræp 'myuzɪk/

Magazine 3

chocolate /'tʃaklɪt/
freeze /friz/
steal /'stiəl/

Unit 10

Parties

decorate the room /'dekə,reit ðe rʊm/
eat cake /it keik/
give a concert /gɪv ə 'kan,sərt/
give presents /gɪv 'prezənts/
make a cake /meik ə keik/
make cards /meik kardz/
play CDs /plei ,si'diz/
wear nice clothes /wer nais klouz/

Leisure activities

go out with friends /gou aut wɪð frendz/
go shopping /gou ʃapɪŋ/
go swimming /gou swimɪŋ/
go to the library /gou tə ðe 'lai,breri/
play a team sport /plei ə tim spɔrt/
play computer games /plei kəm'pyutər geimz/
read books /rid bʊkz/
surf the Net /sərf ðe net/
talk on the phone /tɔk an ðe foun/
watch TV /watʃ ,ti'vi/

Living English

cheerleader /tʃɪrlidər/
competition /,kampə'tiʃən/
karaoke /'kærioki/
snow /snou/

Review 5

camp /kæmp/

Unit 11

Actions

closing /klousɪŋ/
dropping /drapɪŋ/
falling /fɔlɪŋ/
laughing /læfɪŋ/
opening /'oupənɪŋ/
pulling /pʊlɪŋ/
pushing /pʊʃɪŋ/
shouting /ʃautɪŋ/

Rooms in a house

bathroom /bæθrum, rʊm/
bedroom /bedrum, rʊm/
dining room /dainɪŋ rum, rʊm/
kitchen /'kɪtʃən/
living room /'lɪvɪŋ rum, rʊm/
yard /yard/

Other

photo album /foutou 'ælbəm/
play the violin /plei ðe ,vaiə'lɪn/
throw /θrou/
towel /'tauəl/

Unit 12

Actions

carry /'kæri/
exchange /ɪks'tʃeindʒ/
follow /'falou/
make a phone call /meik ə foun kɔl/
shake hands /ʃeik hændz/
wave /weiv/

Clothes

boots /butz/
glasses /glæsiz/
jacket /'dzækɪt/
pants /pæntz/
shirt /ʃərt/
shoes /ʃuz/
skirt /skərt/
sunglasses /sənglæsiz/
briefcase /brifkeis/
shopping bag /ʃapɪŋ bæg/

Other

money /'məni/
suspect /sə'spekt/

Magazine 4

balloons /bə'lunz/
dramas /'draməz, 'dræməz/
game show /geim ʃou/
news program /nuz 'prou,græm/
police show /pə'lis ʃou/
reality TV /ri'æləti ʃou/
science /'saiəns/